COLLECTED POEMS

Also by Gillian Clarke from Carcanet

The King of Britain's Daughter
Selected Poems

GILLIAN CLARKE

COLLECTED POEMS

CARCANET

First published in 1997 by
Carcanet Press Limited
4th Floor, Conavon Court
12-16 Blackfriars Street
Manchester M3 5BQ

A CIP catalogue record for this book
is available from the British Library
ISBN 1 85754 335 1

The publisher acknowledges financial assistance
from the Arts Council of England

Set in 10 pt Horley Old Style by Bryan Williamson, Frome
Printed and bound in England by SRP Ltd, Exeter

Contents

from *The King of Britain's Daughter*

from

The Sundial

The Sundial

Owain was ill today. In the night
He was delirious, shouting of lions
In the sleepless heat. Today, dry
And pale, he took a paper circle,
Laid it on the grass which held it
With curling fingers. In the still
Centre he pushed the broken bean
Stick, gathering twelve fragments
Of stone, placed them at measured
Distances. Then he crouched, slightly
Trembling with fever, calculating
The mathematics of sunshine.

He looked up, his eyes dark,
Intelligently adult as though
The wave of fever taught silence
And immobility for the first time.
Here, in his enforced rest, he found
Deliberation, and the slow finger
Of light, quieter than night lions,
More worthy of his concentration.
All day he told the time to me.
All day we felt and watched the sun
Caged in its white diurnal heat,
Pointing at us with its black stick.

Journey

As far as I am concerned
We are driving into oblivion.
On either side there is nothing,
And beyond your driving
Shaft of light it is black.
You are a miner digging
For a future, a mineral
Relationship in the dark.
I can hear the darkness drip

From the other world where people
Might be sleeping, might be alive.

Certainly there are white
Gates with churns waiting
For morning, their cream standing.
Once we saw an old table
Standing square on the grass verge.
Our lamps swept it clean, shook
The crumbs into the hedge and left it.
A tractor too, beside a load
Of logs, bringing from a deeper
Dark a damp whiff of the fungoid
Sterility of the conifers.

Complacently I sit, swathed
In sleepiness. A door shuts
At the end of a dark corridor.
Ahead not a cat's eye winks
To deceive us with its green
Invitation. As you hurl us
Into the black contracting
Chasm, I submit like a blind
And folded baby, being born.

Snow on the Mountain

There was a girl riding a white pony
Which seemed an elemental part
Of the snow. A crow cut a clean line
Across the hill, which we grasped as a rope
To pull us up the pale diagonal.

The point was to be first at the top
Of the mountain. Our laughter bounced far
Below us like five fists full of pebbles. About us
Lay the snow, deep in the hollows,
Very clean and dry, untouched.

I arrived breathless, my head breaking
The surface of the glittering light, thinking
No place could claim more beauty, white
Slag tips like cones of sugar spun
By the pit wheels under Machen mountain.

I sat on a rock in the sun, watching
My snowboys play. Pit villages shine
Like anthracite. Completed, the pale rider
Rode away. I turned to him and saw
His joy fall like the laughter down a dark
Crack. The black crow shadowed him.

Blaen Cwrt

You ask how it is. I will tell you.
There is no glass. The air spins in
The stone rectangle. We warm our hands
With apple wood. Some of the smoke
Rises against the ploughed, brown field
As a sign to our neighbours in the
Four folds of the valley that we are in.
Some of the smoke seeps through the stones
Into the barn where it curls like fern
On the walls. Holding a thick root
I press my bucket through the surface
Of the water, lift it brimming and skim
The leaves away. Our fingers curl on
Enamel mugs of tea, like ploughmen.
The stones clear in the rain
Giving their colours. It's not easy.
There are no brochure blues or boiled sweet
Reds. All is ochre and earth and cloud-green
Nettles tasting sour and the smells of moist
Earth and sheep's wool. The wattle and daub
Chimney hood has decayed away, slowly
Creeping to dust, chalking the slate
Floor with stories. It has all the first
Necessities for a high standard

Of civilised living: silence inside
A circle of sound, water and fire,
Light on uncountable miles of mountain
From a big, unpredictable sky,
Two rooms, waking and sleeping,
Two languages, two centuries of past
To ponder on, and the basic need
To work hard in order to survive.

Baby-sitting

I am sitting in a strange room listening
For the wrong baby. I don't love
This baby. She is sleeping a snuffly
Roseate, bubbling sleep; she is fair;
She is a perfectly acceptable child.
I am afraid of her. If she wakes
She will hate me. She will shout
Her hot midnight rage, her nose
Will stream disgustingly and the perfume
Of her breath will fail to enchant me.

To her I will represent absolute
Abandonment. For her it will be worse
Than for the lover cold in lonely
Sheets; worse than for the woman who waits
A moment to collect her dignity
Beside the bleached bone in the terminal ward.
As she rises sobbing from the monstrous land
Stretching for milk-familiar comforting,
She will find me and between us two
It will not come. It will not come.

Calf

On the hottest, stillest day of the summer
A calf was born in a field
At Pant-y-Cetris; two buzzards
Measured the volume of the sky;
The hills brimmed with incoming
Night. In the long grass we could see
The cow, her sides heaving, a focus
Of restlessness in the complete calm,
Her calling at odds with silence.

The light flowed out leaving stars
And clarity. Hot and slippery, the scalding
Baby came, and the cow stood up, her cool
Flanks like white flowers in the dark.
We waited while the calf struggled
To stand, moved as though this
Were the first time. I could feel the soft sucking
Of the new-born, the tugging pleasure
Of bruised reordering, the signal
Of milk's incoming tide, and satisfaction
Fall like a clean sheet around us.

Nightride

The road unwinding under our wheels
New in the headlamps like a roll of foil.
The rain is a recorder writing tunes
In telegraph wires, kerbs and cats' eyes,
Reflections and the lights of little towns.

He turns his head to look at me.
'Why are you quiet?' Shiny road rhythm,
Rain rhythm, beat of the windscreen wipers,
I push my knee against his in the warmth
And the car thrusts the dark and rain away.

The child sleeps, and I reflect, as I breathe
His brown hair, and watch the apple they gave him
Held in his hot hands, that a tree must ache
With the sweet weight of the round rosy fruit,
As I with Dylan's head, nodding on its stalk.

Catrin

I can remember you, child,
As I stood in a hot, white
Room at the window watching
The people and cars taking
Turn at the traffic lights.
I can remember you, our first
Fierce confrontation, the tight
Red rope of love which we both
Fought over. It was a square
Environmental blank, disinfected
Of paintings or toys. I wrote
All over the walls with my
Words, coloured the clean squares
With the wild, tender circles
Of our struggle to become
Separate. We want, we shouted,
To be two, to be ourselves.

Neither won nor lost the struggle
In the glass tank clouded with feelings
Which changed us both. Still I am fighting
You off, as you stand there
With your straight, strong, long
Brown hair and your rosy,
Defiant glare, bringing up
From the heart's pool that old rope,
Tightening about my life,
Trailing love and conflict,
As you ask may you skate
In the dark, for one more hour.

Still Life

It was good tonight
To polish brass with you,
Our hands slightly gritty
With Brasso, as they would feel
If we'd been in the sea, salty.
It was as if we burnished
Our friendship, polished it
Until all the light-drowning
Tarnish of deceit
Were stroked away. Patterns
Of incredible honesty
Delicately grew, revealed
Quite openly to the pressure
Of the soft, torn rag.
We made a yellow-gold
Still-life out of clocks,
Candlesticks and kettles.
My sadness puzzled you.
I rubbed the full curve
Of an Indian goblet,
Feeling its illusory
Heat. It cooled beneath
My fingers and I read
In the braille formality
Of pattern, in the leaf
And tendril and stylised tree,
That essentially each
Object remains cold,
Separate, only reflecting
The other's warmth.

Storwm Awst

The cat walks. It listens, as I do,
To the wind which leans its iron
Shoulders on our door. Neither
The purr of a cat nor my blood
Runs smoothly for elemental fear
Of the storm. This then is the big weather
They said was coming. All the signs
Were bad, the gulls coming in white,
Lapwings gathering, the sheep too
Calling all night. The gypsies
Were making their fires in the woods
Down there in the east . . . always
A warning. The rain stings, the whips
Of the laburnum hedge lash the roof
Of the cringing cottage. A curious
Calm, coming from the storm, unites
Us, as we wonder if the work
We have done will stand. Will the tyddyn,[1]
In its group of strong trees on the high
Hill, hold against the storwm Awst[2]
Running across hills where everything
Alive listens, pacing its house, heart still?

Death of a Young Woman

She died on a hot day. In a way
Nothing was different. The stretched white
Sheet of her skin tightened no further.
She was fragile as a yacht before,
Floating so still on the blue day's length,
That one would not know when the breath

---

[1]   tyddyn : smallholding (Welsh)
[2]   storwm Awst : August storm (Welsh)

Blew out and the sail finally slackened.
Her eyes had looked opaquely in the
Wrong place to find those who smiled
From the bedside, and for a long time
Our conversations were silent.

The difference was that in her house
The people were broken by her loss.
He wept for her and for the hard tasks
He had lovingly done, for the short,
Fierce life she had lived in the white bed,
For the burden he had put down for good.
As we sat huddled in pubs supporting
Him with beer and words' warm breath,
We felt the hollowness of his release.
Our own ungrateful health prowled, young,
Gauche about her death. He was polite,
Isolated. Free. No point in going home.

Swinging

At the end of the hot day it rains
Softly, stirring the smells from the raked
Soil. In her sundress and shorts she rocks
On the swing, watching the rain run down
Her brown arms, hands folded warm between
Small thighs, watching her white daps darken
And soak in the cut and sodden grass.

She used to fling her anguish into
My arms, staining my solitude with
Her salt and grimy griefs. Older now
She runs, her violence prevailing
Against silence and the Avenue's
Complacency, I her hatred's object.

Her dress, the washed green of deck chairs, sun
Bleached and chalk-sea rinsed, colours the drops,
And her hair a flag, half and then full
Mast in the apple-trees, flies in the face
Of the rain. Raised now her hands grip tight
The iron rods, her legs thrusting the tide
Of rain aside until, parallel
With the sky, she triumphs and gently
Falls. A green kite. I wind in the string.

Lunchtime Lecture

And this from the second or third millenium
B.C., a female, aged about twenty-two.
A white, fine skull, full up with darkness
As a shell with sea, drowned in the centuries.
Small, perfect. The cranium would fit the palm
Of a man's hand. Some plague or violence
Destroyed her, and her whiteness lay safe in a shroud
Of silence, undisturbed, unrained on, dark
For four thousand years. Till a tractor in summer
Biting its way through the longcairn for supplies
Of stone, broke open the grave and let a crowd of light
Stare in at her, and she stared quietly back.

As I look at her I feel none of the shock
The farmer felt as, unprepared, he found her.
Here in the Museum, like death in hospital,
Reasons are given, labels, causes, catalogues.
The smell of death is done. Left, only her bone
Purity, the light and shade beauty that her man
Was denied sight of, the perfect edge of the place
Where the pieces join, with no mistakes, like boundaries.

She's a tree in winter, stripped white on a black sky,
Leafless formality, brow, bough in fine relief.
I, at some other season, illustrate the tree
Fleshed, with woman's hair and colours and the rustling
Blood, the troubled mind that she has overthrown.
We stare at each other, dark into sightless
Dark, seeing only ourselves in the black pools,
Gulping the risen sea that booms in the shell.

Dyddgu Replies to Dafydd 1

All year in open places, underneath
    the frescoed forest ceiling,
    we have made ceremony
    out of this seasonal love.

Dividing the lead-shade as divers white
    in green pools we rose to dry
    islands of sudden sun. Then
    love seemed generosity.

Original sin I whitened from your
    mind, my colours influenced
    your flesh, as sun on the floor
    and warm furniture of a church.

So did our season bloom in mild weather,
    reflected gold like butter
    under chins, repeatedly
    unfolding to its clock of seed.

Autumn, our forest room is growing cold.
    I wait, shivering, feeling a
    dropping sun, a coming dark,
    your heart changing the subject.

---

[1]   Dafydd ap Gwilym: Fourteenth-century Welsh poet; Dyddgu, one of the
two women to whom he addressed love poems.

The season coughs as it falls, like a coal;
    the trees ache. The forest falls
    to ruin, a roofless minster
    where only two still worship.

Love still, like sun, a vestment, celebrates,
    its warmth about our shoulders.
    I dread the day when Dyddgu's once
    loved name becomes a common cloak.

Your touch is not so light. I grow heavy.
    I wait too long, grow anxious,
    note your changing gestures, fear
    desire's alteration.

The winter stars are flying and the owls
    sing. You are packing your songs
    in a sack, narrowing your
    words, as you stare at the road.

The feet of young men beat, somewhere far off
    on the mountain. I would women
    had roads to tread in winter
    and other lovers waiting.

A raging rose all summer falls to snow,
    keeps its continuance in
    frozen soil. I must be patient
    for the breaking of the crust.

I must be patient that you will return
    when the wind whitens the tender
    underbelly of the March grass
    thick as pillows under the oaks.

At Ystrad Fflûr [1]

No way of flowers at this late season.
  Only a river blossoming on stone
  and the mountain ash in fruit.

All rivers are young in these wooded hills
  where the abbey watches and the young Teifi
  counts her rosary on stones.

I cross by a simple bridge constructed
  of three slim trees. Two lie across. The third
  is a broken balustrade.

The sun is warm after rain on the red
  pelt of the slope, fragmentary through trees
  like torches in the dark.

They have been here before me and have seen
  the sun's lunulae in the profound
  quietness of water.

The Teifi is in full flood and rich
  with metals: a torc in a brown pool
  gleaming for centuries.

I am spellbound in a place of spells. Cloud
  changes gold to stone as their circled bones
  dissolve in risen corn.

The river races for the south too full
  of summer rain for safety, spilt water
  whitening low-lying fields.

From oak and birchwoods through the turning trees
  where leaf and hour and century fall
  seasonally, desire runs

---

[1]   The burial place of Dafydd ap Gwilym

Like sparks in stubble through the memory
of the place, and a yellow mustard field
is a sheet of flame in the heart.

Railway Tracks

When you talk to me of carrots fresh pulled
From your grandfather's allotment, how he
Would wash the soil away in the green rain
Of the water butt, and then shake them dry;
When I see you carry your fruit away
To the railway bank, and feast there neck high
In golden, seeded grass and flowering weeds,
I see my own mysterious railway track,
Ragwort, dog daisies and valerian
Swim in the great heat on the waves of grass.
Sweet surreptitious smells, like tar and sweat,
And dusty arms, and pollen on my knees.
A vast, dead brick building with a hundred
Broken windows, the track losing its way
Besieged by leaf and stalk and flowerhead
Triumphant to be brought again to their
Own country. Above all, leaping from sleeper
To sleeper, along these lines that lead deep
And parallel into the wilderness,
I hear another footfall follow mine.

But who that child was, what the happiness,
And where the track, no one can tell me now.
It was as good as carrots on the bank
To find a place where wildness had returned.
The old, blind warehouse, full of swooping birds,
Has given me a taste for dereliction,
For the fall of towers, the rot of stone and brick,
For the riot of the ragged weed's return,
The reinstatement of the wilderness.

Foghorns

When Catrin was a small child
She thought the foghorn moaning
Far out at sea was the sad
Solitary voice of the moon
Journeying to England.
She heard it warn 'Moon, Moon',
As it worked the Channel, trading
Weather like rags and bones.

Tonight, after the still sun
And the silent heat, as haze
Became rain and weighed glistening
In brimful leaves, and the last bus
Splashes and fades with a soft
Wave-sound, the foghorns moan, moon-
Lonely and the dry lawns drink.
The dimmed moon, calling still,
Hauls sea-rags through the streets.

Curlew

She dips her bill in the rim of the sea.
Her beak is the ellipse
of a world much smaller
than that far section of the sea's
circumference. A curve enough to calculate
the field's circle and its heart
of eggs in the cold grass.

All day while I scythed my territory
out of nettles, laid claim to my cantref,
she has cut her share of sky. Her song bubbles
long as a plane trail from her savage mouth.
I clean the blade with newspaper. Dusk blurs

circle within circle till there's nothing left
but the egg pulsing in the dark against her ribs.
For each of us the possessed space contracts
to the nest's heat, the blood's small circuit.

Burning Nettles

Where water springs, pools, waits
Collection in a bucket
In the late summer heat,
Beech trees observe foresight
Of autumn wrinkling their leaves.
The cold will wither this
Old garden. The plumpness shrinks
Beneath its skin, a light
Frown puckers the mirrored sky.

The scythe bleeds ancient herbs
Whose odours come as ghosts
To disturb memory.
My fire of nettles crackles
Like bees creeping in a green
Hive, making white smoke from weeds,
And the strange, sweet plants Marged
Sowed, or Nanu, before
The wind changed from the east.

With the reaping hook blade
I lift an exhausted moth
From the hot mound. It lives
To die of cold. Inside the cave
Of thatched grass the secret fire
Thrives on my summer. Nettles
Turn to ashes in its heart,
Crucible of the fragrant and
The sour. Only soil survives.

Rose bay willowherb, ragwort,
Grass, disintegrate and make
A white continuous mane
For the mountain. Ponies turn
Windward. The evening's heat
Belies the beech tree's shiver,
And pinpoints of ice on skin
Are nettlestings, not rain. Fire,
Buried in flower-heads, makes
Bright ritual of decay,
Transubstantiates the green
Leaf to fertility.

Last Rites

During this summer of the long drought
The road to Synod Inn has kept
Its stigmata of dust and barley-seed;

At the inquest they tell it again:
How the lorry tents us from the sun,
His pulse dangerous in my hands,
A mains hum only, no message
Coming through. His face warm, profiled
Against tarmac, the two-stroke Yamaha
Dead as a black horse in a war.
Only his hair moves and the sound
Of the parched grass and harebells a handspan
Away, his fear still with me like the scream
Of a jet in an empty sky.
I cover him with the grey blanket
From my bed, touch his face as a child
Who makes her favourite cosy.
His blood on my hands, his cariad[1] in my arms.

---

[1]   cariad: darling (Welsh)

Driving her home we share that vision
Over August fields dying of drought
Of the summer seas shattering
At every turn of Cardigan Bay
Under the cruel stones of the sun.

Harvest at Mynachlog

At last the women come with baskets,
The older one in flowered apron,
A daisied cloth covering the bread
And dappled china, sweet tea
In a vast can. The women stoop
Spreading their cups in the clover.

The engines stop. A buzzard watches
From the fence. We bury our wounds
In the deep grass: sunburnt shoulders,
Bodies scratched with straw, wrists bruised
From the weight of the bales, blood beating.

For hours the baler has been moulding
Golden bricks from the spread straw,
Spewing them at random in the stubble.
I followed the slow load, heaved each
Hot burden, feeling the sun contained.

And unseen over me a man leaned,
Taking the weight to make the toppling
Load. Then the women came, friendly
And cool as patches of flowers at the far
Field edge, mothy and blurred in the heat.

We are soon recovered and roll over
In the grass to take our tea. We talk
Of other harvests. They remember
How a boy, flying his plane so low
Over the cut fields that his father

Straightened from his work to wave his hat
At the boasting sky, died minutes later
On an English cliff, in such a year
As this, the barns brimming gold.

We are quiet again, holding our cups
In turn for the tilting milk, sad, hearing
The sun roar like a rush of grain
Engulfing all winged things that live
One moment in the eclipsing light.

Clywedog

The people came out in pairs,
Old, most of them, holding their places
Close till the very last minute,
Even planting the beans as usual
That year, grown at last accustomed
To the pulse of the bulldozers.
High in those uphill gardens, scarlet
Beanflowers blazed hours after
The water rose in the throats of the farms.

Only the rooted things stayed:
The wasted hay, the drowned
Dog roses, the farms, their kitchens silted
With their own stones, hedges
And walls a thousand years old.
And the mountains, in a head-collar
Of flood, observe a desolation
They'd grown used to before the coming
Of the wall-makers. Language
Crumbles to wind and bird-call.

Choughs

I follow you downhill to the edge
My feet taking as naturally as yours
To a sideways tread, finding footholds
Easily in the turf, accustomed
As we are to a sloping country.

The cliffs buttress the bay's curve to the north
And here drop sheer and sudden to the sea.
The choughs plummet from sight then ride
The updraught of the cliffs' mild yellow
Light, fold, fall with closed wings from the sky.

At the last moment as in unison they turn
A ripcord of the wind is pulled in time.
He gives her food and the saliva
Of his red mouth, draws her black feathers, sweet
As shining grass across his bill.

Rare birds that pair for life. There they go
Divebombing the marbled wave a yard
Above the spray. Wings flick open
A stoop away
From the drawn teeth of the sea.

St Thomas's Day

It's the darkest morning of the year.
Day breaks in water runnels
In the yard: a flutter
Of light on a tiled roof;
The loosening of night's
Stonehold on tap and bolt.

Rain on my face wakes me
From recent sleep. I cross
The yard, shovel bumping
In the barrow, fingers
Stiff as hinges. Catrin
Brings bran and fresh hay.

A snort in the dark, a shove
For supremacy.
My hands are warmed
In the steam of his welcome.
Midwinter, only here
Do the fields still summer,
Thistlehead and flower
Powdered by hoof and tooth.

from

Letter from a Far Country

White Roses

Outside the green velvet sitting room
white roses bloom after rain.
They hold water and sunlight
like cups of fine white china.

Within the boy who sleeps in my care
in the big chair the cold bloom
opens at terrible speed
and the splinter of ice moves

in his blood as he stirs in the chair.
Remembering me he smiles
politely, gritting his teeth
in silence on pain's red blaze.

A stick man in the ashes, his fires
die back. He is spars and springs.
He can talk again, gather
his cat to his bones. She springs

with a small cry in her throat, kneading
with diamond paws his dry
as tinder flesh. The least spark
of pain will burn him like straw.

The sun carelessly shines after rain.
The cat tracks thrushes in sweet
dark soil. And without concern
the rose outlives the child.

Return to Login

Chapel and bridge. A headlong fall
into woods. A river running fast
divides the wild cow parsley.
'My father lived here once,' I said,
'I think you knew him.'

The sun, hot at our backs, whitens
the lane. She, in shadow, allows
the sun to pass her into the passage.
I gain entry at his name, tea,
a lace cloth on the table.

When talking is done she ruffles
my son's brown hair with a hand
that is bruised with age. Veins stand,
fast water in her wrists. Handshakes,
glances converging could not span
such giddy water.

Out in the lane the thrush outsings
the river. The village is at lunch.
The bridge burns with cow parsley.
We stand in the brilliance without words,
watch him running into the light.

Should he turn now to wave and wait
for me, where sunlight concentrates
blindingly on the bridge, he'd see
all this in sepia, hear footsteps
not yet taken fade away.

Miracle on St David's Day

'They flash upon that inward eye
Which is the bliss of solitude'
    The Daffodils by W. Wordsworth

An afternoon yellow and open-mouthed
with daffodils. The sun treads the path
among cedars and enormous oaks.
It might be a country house, guests strolling,
the rumps of gardeners between nursery shrubs.

I am reading poetry to the insane.
An old woman, interrupting, offers
as many buckets of coal as I need.
A beautiful chestnut-haired boy listens
entirely absorbed. A schizophrenic

on a good day, they tell me later.
In a cage of first March sun a woman
sits not listening, not seeing, not feeling.
In her neat clothes the woman is absent.
A big, mild man is tenderly led

to his chair. He has never spoken.
His labourer's hands on his knees, he rocks
gently to the rhythms of the poems.
I read to their presences, absences,
to the big, dumb labouring man as he rocks.

He is suddenly standing, silently,
huge and mild, but I feel afraid. Like slow
movement of spring water or the first bird
of the year in the breaking darkness,
the labourer's voice recites 'The Daffodils'.

The nurses are frozen, alert; the patients
seem to listen. He is hoarse but word-perfect.
Outside the daffodils are still as wax,
a thousand, ten thousand, their syllables
unspoken, their creams and yellows still.

Forty years ago, in a Valleys school,
the class recited poetry by rote.
Since the dumbness of misery fell
he has remembered there was a music
of speech and that once he had something to say.

When he's done, before the applause, we observe
the flowers' silence. A thrush sings
and the daffodils are flame.

East Moors

At the end of a bitter April
the cherries flower at last in Penylan.
Beyond the blossoming city
where the steelworks used to smoke,
is a flash of sea with two blue islands.

I live in the house I was born in,
am accustomed to the sudden glow
of flame in the night sky, the dark sound
of something heavy dropped, miles off,
the smell of sulphur almost natural.

In Roath and Rumney now, washing strung
down the narrow gardens will stay clean.
Lethargy settles in front rooms and wives
have lined up little jobs for men to do.
At East Moors they've closed the steelworks.

A few men stay to see it through –
theirs the bitterest time
as rolling mills make rubble.
Demolition gangs erase skylines
whose hieroglyphs recorded all our stories.

I am reminded of that Sunday years ago
when we brought the children to watch
two water cooling towers blown up,
recall the void in the sunlight,
like a death.

On this first day of May
an icy rain is blowing through this town,
quieter, cleaner, poorer from today.
The cherries are in flower in Penylan,
and over East Moors the sky whitens, blind.

Scything

It is blue May. There is work
to be done. The spring's eye blind
with algae, the stopped water
silent. The garden fills
with nettle and briar.
Dylan drags branches away.
I wade forward with my scythe.

There is stickiness on the blade.
Yolk on my hands. Albumen and blood.
Fragments of shell are baby-bones,
the scythe a scalpel, bloodied and guilty
with crushed feathers, mosses, the cut cords
of the grass. We shout at each other
each hurting with a separate pain.

From the crown of the hawthorn tree
to the ground the willow warbler
drops. All day in silence she repeats
her question. I too return
to the place holding the pieces,
at first still hot from the knife,
recall how warm birth fluids are.

Jac Codi Baw [1]

They have torn down in the space of time
it takes to fill a shopping bag,
the building that stood beside my car.
It was grown over with ragwort,
toadflax and buddleia, windows
blind with boarding. Other cars
had time to drive away. Mine
is splattered with the stones' blood, smoky
with ghosts. We are used to the slow
change that weather brings, the gradual
death of a generation, old bricks
crumbling. Inside the car dust lies,
grit in my eyes, in my hair.

He doesn't care. It's a joke to him
clearing space for the pile-drivers,
cheerful in his yellow machine,
cat-calling, laughing at my grief.
But for him too the hand-writing
of a city will be erased.
I can't laugh. Too much comes down
in the deaths of warehouses. Brickdust,
shards of Caernarfon slate. Blood on our hands.

---

[1]   Jac Codi Baw: J.C.B.: Jack Dig Dirt

Ram

He died privately.
His disintegration is quiet.
Grass grows among the stems of his ribs,
Ligaments unpicked by the slow rain.
The birds dismantled him from spring nests.
He has spilled himself on the marsh,
His evaporations and his seepings,
His fluids filled a reservoir.
Not long since he could have come
Over the Saddle[1] like a young moon,
His cast shadow whitening Breconshire.

The blue of his eyes is harebell.
Mortality gapes in the craters of his face.
Buzzards cry in the cave of his skull
And a cornucopia of lambs is bleating
Down the Fan[1] of his horns.
In him more of October than rose hips
And bitter sloes. The wind cries drily
Down his nostril bones. The amber
Of his horizontal eye
Is light on reservoir, raven
In winter sky. The sun that creams
The buzzard's belly as she treads air
Whitens his forehead. Flesh
Blackens in the scrolls of his nostrils,
Something of him lingering in bone
Corridors catches my throat.

Seeking a vessel for blackberries and sloes
This helmet would do, were it not filled
Already with its own blacks,
Night in the socket of his eye.

---

[1] Saddle and Fan: parts of the Brecon Beacon mountains

Buzzard

No sutures in the steep brow
of this cranium, as in mine
or yours. Delicate ellipse
as smooth as her own egg

or the cleft flesh of a fruit.
From the plundered bones on the hill,
like a fire in its morning ashes,
you guess it's a buzzard's skull.

You carry it gently home,
hoping no Last Day of the birds
will demand assembly
of her numerous white parts.

In the spaces we can't see
on the other side of walls
as fine as paper, brain and eye
dry out under the gossamers.

Between the sky and the mouse
that moves at the barley field's
spinning perimeter, only
a mile of air and the ganging

crows, their cries stones at her head.
In death, the last stoop, all's risked.
She scorns the scavengers
who feed on death, and never

feel the lightning flash of heart
dropping on heart, warm fur, blood.

Friesian Bull

He blunders through the last dream
of the night. I hear him, waking.
A brick and concrete stall, narrow
as a heifer's haunches. Steel bars
between her trap and his small yard.
A froth of slobbered hay droops
from the stippled muzzle. In the slow
rolling mass of his skull his eyes
surface like fish bellies.

He is chained while they swill his floor.
His stall narrows to rage. He knows
the sweet smell of a heifer's fear.
Remembered summer haysmells reach him,
a trace of the herd's freedom, clover-
loaded winds. The thundering speed
blows up the Dee breathing of plains,
of cattle wading in shallows.
His crazy eyes churn with their vision.

Sunday

Getting up early on a Sunday morning
leaving them sleep for the sake of peace,
the lunch pungent, windows open
for a blackbird singing in Cyncoed.
Starlings glistening in the gutter come
for seed. I let the cats in from the night,
their fur already glossed and warm with March.
I bring the milk, newspaper, settle here
in the bay of the window to watch people
walking to church for Mothering Sunday.
A choirboy holds his robes over his shoulder.
The cats jump up on windowsills to wash
and tremble at the starlings. Like peaty water

sun slowly fills the long brown room.
Opening the paper I admit to this
the war-shriek and starved stare
of a warning I can't name.

Taid's Funeral

From a drawer, a scrap of creased cloth,
an infant's dress of yellowed Viyella
printed with daisies. And a day opens
suddenly as light. The sun is hot.
Grass grows cleanly to a chapel wall.
The stones are rough as a sheepdog's tongue
on the skin of a two-year child.
They allow a fistful of white
gravel, chain her wrists with daisies.

Under the yew tree they lay Taid[1]
in his box like a corm in the ground.

The lawn-mowers are out. Fears repeat
in a conversation of mirrors,
doll within doll; and that old man too small
at last to see, perfect, distinct as a seed.
My hands are cut by silver gravel.
There are dark incisions in the stalks
of the daisies made by a woman's nail.
A new dress stains green with their sap.

---

[1]   Taid: Grandfather (Welsh)

Letter from a Far Country

They have gone. The silence resettles
slowly as dust on the sunlit
surfaces of the furniture.
At first the skull itself makes
sounds in any fresh silence,
a big sea running in a shell.
I can hear my blood rise and fall.

Dear husbands, fathers, forefathers,
this is my apologia, my
letter home from the future,
my bottle in the sea which might
take a generation to arrive.

The morning's all activity.
I draw the detritus of a family's
loud life before me, a snow plough,
a road-sweeper with my cart of leaves.
The washing-machine drones
in the distance. From time to time
as it falls silent I fill baskets
with damp clothes and carry them
into the garden, hang them out,
stand back, take pleasure counting
and listing what I have done.
The furniture is brisk with polish.
On the shelves in all of the rooms
I arrange the books
in alphabetical order
according to subject: Mozart,
Advanced Calculus, William
and Paddington Bear.
Into the drawers I place your clean
clothes, pyjamas with buttons
sewn back on, shirts stacked neatly
under their labels on the shelves.

The chests and cupboards are full,
the house sweet as a honeycomb.
I move in and out of the hive

all day, harvesting, ordering.
You will find all in its proper place,
when I have gone.

As I write I am far away.
First see a landscape. Hill country,
essentially feminine,
the sea not far off. Bryn Isaf
down there in the crook of the hill
under Calfaria's single eye.
My grandmother might have lived there.
Any farm. Any chapel.
Father and minister, on guard,
close the white gates to hold her.

A stony track turns between
ancient hedges, narrowing,
like a lane in a child's book.
Its perspective makes the heart restless
like the boy in the rhyme, his stick
and cotton bundle on his shoulder.

The minstrel boy to the war has gone.
But the girl stays. To mind things.
She must keep. And wait. And pass time.

There's always been time on our hands.
We read this perfectly white page
for the black head of the seal,
for the cormorant, as suddenly gone
as a question from the mind,
snaking underneath the surfaces.
A cross of gull shadow on the sea
as if someone stepped on its grave.
After an immeasurable space
the cormorant breaks the surface
as a small, black, returning doubt.

From here the valley is narrow,
the lane lodged like a halfway ledge.
From the opposite wood the birds
ring like a tambourine. It's not

the birdsong of a garden, thrush
and blackbird, robin and finch,
distinguishable, taking turn.
The song's lost in saps and seepings,
amplified by hollow trees,
cupped leaves and wind in the branches.
All their old conversations
collected carefully, faded
and difficult to read, yet held
forever as voices in a well.

Reflections and fallen stones; shouts
into the scared dark of lead-mines;
the ruined warehouse where the owls stare;
sea-caves; cellars; the back stairs
behind the chenille curtain;
the landing when the lights are out;
nightmares in hot feather beds;
the barn where I'm sent to fetch Taid[1];
that place where the Mellte flows
boldly into limestone caves
and leaps from its hole a mile on,
the nightmare still wild in its voice.

When I was a child a young boy
was drawn into a pipe and drowned
at the swimming pool. I never
forgot him, and pity rivers
inside mountains, and the children
of Hamlyn sucked in by music.
You can hear children crying
from the empty woods.
It's all given back in concert
with the birds and leaves and water
and the song and dance of the Piper.

Listen! to the starlings glistening
on a March morning! Just one day
after snow, an hour after frost,
the thickening grass begins to shine
already in the opening light.

---

[1]   Taid: grandfather (North Wales)

There's wind to rustle the blood,
the sudden flame of crocus.

My grandmother might be standing
in the great silence before the Wars,
hanging the washing between trees
over the white and the red hens.
Sheets. Threadworked pillowcases.
Mamgu's[1] best pais[2]. Her Sunday frock.

The sea stirs restlessly between
the sweetness of clean sheets,
the lifted arms,
the rustling petticoats.

My mother's laundry list, ready
on Mondays when the van called.
The rest soaked in glutinous starch
and whitened with a bluebag
kept in a broken cup.

(In the airing cupboard you'll see
a map, numbering and placing
every towel, every sheet.
I have charted all your needs.)

It has always been a matter
of lists. We have been counting,
folding, measuring, making,
tenderly laundering cloth
ever since we have been women.

The waves are folded meticulously,
perfectly white. Then they are tumbled
and must come to be folded again.

Four herring gulls and their shadows
are shouting at the clear glass
of a shaken wave. The sea's a sheet

---

[1] Mamgu: grandmother (South Wales)

[2] pais: petticoat (Welsh)

bellying in the wind, snapping.
Air and white linen. Our airing cupboards
are full of our satisfactions.

The gulls grieve at our contentment.
It is a masculine question.
'Where' they call 'are your great works?'
They slip their fetters and fly up
to laugh at land-locked women.
Their cries are cruel as greedy babies.

Our milky tendernesses dry
to crisp lists; immaculate
linen; jars labelled and glossy
with our perfect preserves.
Spiced oranges; green tomato
chutney; Seville orange marmalade
annually staining gold
the snows of January.

(The saucers of marmalade
are set when the amber wrinkles
like the sea if you blow it.)

Jams and jellies of blackberry,
crabapple, strawberry, plum,
greengage and loganberry.
You can see the fruit pressing
their little faces against the glass;
tiny onions imprisoned
in their preservative juices.

Familiar days are stored whole
in bottles. There's a wet morning
orchard in the dandelion wine;
a white spring distilled
in elderflower's clarity;
and a loving, late, sunburning
day of October in syrups
of rose hip and the beautiful
black sloes that stained the gin to rose.

It is easy to make of love
these ceremonials. As priests
we fold cloth, break bread, share wine,
hope there's enough to go round.

(You'll find my inventories pinned
inside all of the cupboard doors).

Soon they'll be planting the barley.
I imagine I see it, stirring
like blown sand, feel the stubble
cutting my legs above blancoed
daps in a summer too hot
for Wellingtons. The cans of tea
swing squeakily on wire loops,
outheld, not to scald myself,
over the ten slow leagues
of the field of golden knives.
To be out with the men, at work,
I had longed to carry their tea,
for the feminine privilege,
for the male right to the field.
Even that small task made me bleed.
Halfway between the flowered lap
of my grandmother and the black
heraldic silhouette of men
and machines on the golden field,
I stood crying, my ankle bones
raw and bleeding like the poppies
trussed in the corn stooks in their torn
red silks and soft mascara blacks.

(The recipe for my best bread,
half granary meal, half strong brown flour,
water, sugar, yeast and salt,
is copied out in the small black book).

In the black book of this parish
a hundred years ago
you will find the unsupported
woman had 'pauper' against her name.
She shared it with old men.

The parish was rich with movement.
The woollen mills were spinning.
Water-wheels milled the sunlight
and the loom's knock was a heart
behind all activity.
The shuttles were quick as birds
in the warp of the oakwoods.
In the fields the knives were out
in a glint of husbandry.
In back bedrooms, barns and hedges,
in hollows of the hills,
the numerous young were born.

The people were at work:
dressmaker; wool carder; quilter;
midwife; farmer; apprentice;
house servant; scholar; labourer;
shepherd; stocking knitter; tailor;
carpenter; mariner; ploughman;
wool spinner; cobbler; cottager;
Independent Minister.

And the paupers: Enoch Elias
and Ann, his wife; David Jones,
Sarah and Esther their daughter;
Mary Evans and Ann Tanrallt;
Annie Cwm March and child;
Eleanor Thomas, widow, Crug Glas;
Sara Jones, 84, and daughter;
Nicholas Rees, aged 80, and his wife;
Mariah Evans the Cwm, widow;
on the parish for want of work.
Housebound by infirmity, age,
widowhood, or motherhood.

Before the Welfare State who cared
for sparrows in a hard spring?

The stream's cleaner now; it idles
past derelict mill-wheels; the drains
do its work. Since the tanker sank
the unfolding rose of the sea

blooms on the beaches, wave on wave
black, track-marked, each tide
a procession of the dead.
Slack water's treacherous; each veined
wave is a stain in seal-milk;
the sea gapes, hopelessly
licking itself.

(Examine your hands
scrupulously
for signs of dirt in your own blood.
And wash them before meals).

In that innocent smallholding
where the swallows live and field mice
winter and the sheep barge in
under the browbone, the windows
are blind, are doors for owls,
bolt-holes for dreams. The thoughts have flown.
The last death was a suicide.
The lowing cows discovered her,
the passing-bell of their need
warned a winter morning that day
when no one came to milk them.
Later, they told me, a baby
was born in the room where she died,
as if by this means sanctified,
a death outcried by a birth.
Middle-aged, poor, isolated,
she could not recover
from mourning an old parent's death.
Influenza brought an hour
too black, too narrow to escape.

More mysterious to them
was the woman who had everything.
A village house with railings;
rooms of good furniture;
fine linen in the drawers;
a garden full of herbs and flowers;
a husband in work; grown sons.
She had a cloud on her mind,

they said, and her death shadowed them.
It couldn't be explained.

I watch for her face looking out,
small and white, from every window,
like a face in a jar. Gossip,
whispers, lowing sounds. Laughter.

The people have always talked.
The landscape collects conversations
as carefully as a bucket,
gives them back in concert
with a wood of birdsong.

(If you hear your name in that talk
don't listen. Eavesdroppers never
heard anything good of themselves).

When least expected you catch
the eye of the enemy
looking coldly from the old world . . .
Here's a woman who ought to be
up to her wrists in marriage;
not content with the second hand
she is shaking the bracelets
from her arms. The sea circles
her ankles. Watch its knots loosen
from the delicate bones
of her feet, from the rope of foam
about a rock. The seal swims
in a collar of water
drawing the horizon in its wake.
And doubt breaks the perfect
white surface of the day.

About the tree in the middle
of the cornfield the loop of gold
is loose as water; as the love
we should bear one another.

When I rock the sea rocks. The moon
doesn't seem to be listening

invisible in a pale sky,
keeping a light hand on the rein.

Where is woman in this trinity?
The mare who draws the load?
The hand on the leather?
The cargo of wheat?

Watching sea-roads I feel
the tightening white currents,
am waterlogged, my time set
to the sea's town clock.
My cramps and drownings, energies,
desires draw the loaded net
of the tide over the stones.

A lap full of pebbles and then
light as a Coca Cola can.
I am freight. I am ship.
I cast ballast overboard.
The moon decides my Equinox.
At high tide I am leaving.

The women are leaving.
They are paying their taxes
and dues. Filling in their passports.
They are paying to Caesar
what is Caesar's, to God what is God's,
To Woman what is Man's.

I hear the dead grandmothers,
Mamgu from Ceredigion,
Nain[1] from the North, all calling
their daughters down from the fields,
calling me in from the road.
They haul at the taut silk cords;
set us fetching eggs, feeding hens,
mixing rage with the family bread,
lock us to the elbows in soap suds.

---

[1]   Nain: grandmother (North Wales)

Their sculleries and kitchens fill
with steam, sweetnesses, goosefeathers.

On the graves of my grandfathers
the stones, in their lichens and mosses,
record each one's importance.
Diaconydd[1]. Trysorydd[2].
Pillars of their society.
Three times at chapel on Sundays.
They are in league with the moon
but as silently stony
as the simple names of their women.

We are hawks trained to return
to the lure from the circle's
far circumference. Children sing
that note that only we can hear.
The baby breaks the waters,
disorders the blood's tune, sets
each filament of the senses
wild. Its cry tugs at flesh, floods
its mother's milky fields.
Nightly in white moonlight I wake
from sleep one whole slow minute
before the hungry child
wondering what woke me.

School's out. The clocks strike four.
Today this letter goes unsigned,
unfinished, unposted.
When it is finished
I will post it from a far country.

If we launch the boat and sail away
Who will rock the cradle? Who will stay?
If women wander over the sea
Who'll be home when you come in for tea?

---

[1]   Diaconydd: deacon
[2]   Trysorydd: treasurer

If we go hunting along with the men
Who will light the fires and bake bread then?
Who'll catch the nightmares and ride them away
If we put to sea and we sail away?

Will the men grow tender and the children strong?
Who will teach the Mam iaith1 and sing them songs?
If we adventure more than a day
Who will do the loving while we're away?

Kingfishers at Condat

Our hair still damp from swimming,
heads full of deep brown water
reflecting with reeds, we drink
an apéritif in Condat.

At the heart of the village silence
of gold-dust and evening heat
the café is full of youths
in leather for motor-cycling.

Their bikes wait in the courtyard,
blue as mallard, glittering flies
taking nourishment from dust,
at rest from their buzzing and fuss.

Excluded, uneasy at their stares
and the outbreak of laughter, we carry
our drinks outside, read their newspaper
in revenge, like a bill of right.

---

[1]   Mam iaith: Mother tongue

Out here on the parapet
the stone has absorbed September.
We sit alone, sweetnesses
of the wine on our mouth and fingers.

Their laughter is distant. The river
moves its surfaces, its reedy
stirrings and sudden glitter
rushing under the bridge.

Downstream the Coly, where we swam,
Meets the Vézère in a wide
confluence, deceivingly
cool under the evening's gold.

The yard is loud with boys. With us
for audience, one by one they go
roaring and glittering into the trees.
The river moves in peace, and there!

under the bank where it's dark, blue
as fire the kingfishers are hunting,
blue as storm, iridescent, alive
to the quoit on the surface

where the fish rises. Dragonfly
blue crackling down the dark vein
of the riverbank, as quick
and as private as joy.

Seamstress at St Léon

As we eat crushed strawberry ice
under a bee-heavy vine
we watch for the seamstress to come.
Through the open doorway we hear
her chatter, see her Singers
glint with gold roses in the dark room.

Embroidery cloths abandoned
at the roadside table; a weir
of lace falls from her chair; silks
spill blossoming from a basket.
Under its turning ribbon of gauze
her tea cools in a white cup.

She sings in the dark interior.
From the sills of the gardenless house
fuchsia and geranium blaze.
Her windows are framed with French knots,
the cracks seeded with lazy daisy.
Her rubber plant reaches the eaves.

Nothing troubles the afternoon dust
or breaks the tenor of bees
but her counterpoint. Out of sight
in their web of scaffolding
under the bridge, workmen whistle
and a hammer rings over water.

A fan of shadow slowly includes us.
Her tea is cold. Imperceptibly
the thicket of roses grows closer.
We make out the sinuous gilding
of sewing machines, vine leaves, stems
and iron tendrils of their treadles.

Lace glimmering at dusk. A foam
of linen, flowers, silences.
Sunlight has flowed from her sills
of yellow stone. Bats are shuttling
their delicate black silks to mesh
that dark doorway on her absence.

Les Grottes

1.

Rouffignac

In the forest overhead
summer fruit is falling
like the beat of a drum.

Hold your breath and you hear
millennia of water
sculpting limestone.

The river runs in the heat
of the sun. We are walking
in its grave, imagine

a throat choking with water.
Vast cupolas
prove its turbulence.

I am not deceived
by the nursery frieze
of mammoth. The circus act

brings on the bison,
black and ochre
ponies on terra cotta.

The Vézère is a ghost,
its footprints everywhere.
Even the kitchen taps

run cloudy into the palms
of our hands, fill our mouths
with chalk.

2.

Font de Gaume

Fourteen thousand years make little difference.
Some of us, finding smooth places in the rough
must carve there, using old water marks.
A stalactite for a horse's thigh, its eye
a fault, or where the river fingered a whorl
a vortex turned the doorways of the skull.
Sinews of calcite, muscles run and slack,
the belly droops, a boulder marbles bone.

The imagination's caverns cry for symbols,
shout to the hot sun in the present tense.
We walk again in the afternoon,
watch out for vipers lazy on their stones.
Two tractors are towing home the harvest.
Tobacco saps evaporate in rows.
The glittering Vézère is at its work,
its inexhaustible calligraphy.

Brother, grinding your colours by tallow light,
I hear your heart beat under my collarbone.

Heron at Port Talbot

Snow falls on the cooling towers
delicately settling on cranes.
Machinery's old bones whiten; death
settles with its rusts, its erosions.

Warning of winds off the sea
the motorway dips to the dock's edge.
My hands tighten on the wheel against
the white steel of the wind.

Then we almost touch, both braking flight,
bank on the air and feel that shocking
intimacy of near-collision,
animal tracks that cross in snow.

I see his living eye, his change of mind,
feel pressure as we bank, the force
of his beauty. We might have died
in some terrible conjunction.

The steel town's sulphurs billow
like dirty washing. The sky stains
with steely inks and fires, chemical
rustings, salt-grains, sand under snow.

And the bird comes, a surveyor
calculating space between old workings
and the mountain hinterland, archangel
come to re-open the heron-roads,

meets me at an inter-section
where wind comes flashing off water
interrupting the warp of the snow
and the broken rhythms of blood.

Suicide on Pentwyn Bridge

I didn't know him,
the man who jumped from the bridge.
But I saw the parabola
of long-drawn-out falling in the brown

eyes of his wife week after week
at the supermarket cash-out.
We would quietly ask 'How is he?'
hear of the hospital's white

care, the corridors between her
and the broken man in the bed,
and the doctors who had no words,
no common supermarket women's talk.

Only after the funeral
I knew how he'd risen, wild
from his chair and told her
he was going out to die.

Very slowly from the first leap
he fell through winter, through the cold
of Christmas, wifely silences,
the blue scare of ambulance,

from his grave on the motorway
to the hospital, two bridges down.
A season later in a slow cortège
he has reached the ground.

Plums

When their time comes they fall
without wind, without rain.
They seep through the trees' muslin
in a slow fermentation.

Daily the low sun warms them
in a late love that is sweeter
than summer. In bed at night
we hear heartbeat of fruitfall.

The secretive slugs crawl home
to the burst honeys, are found
in the morning mouth on mouth,
inseparable.

We spread patchwork counterpanes
for a clean catch. Baskets fill,
never before such harvest,
such a hunters' moon burning

the hawthorns, drunk on syrups
that are richer by night
when spiders pitch
tents in the wet grass.

This morning the red sun
is opening like a rose
on our white wall, prints there
the fishbone shadow of a fern.

The early blackbirds fly
guilty from a dawn haul
of fallen fruit. We too
breakfast on sweetnesses.

Soon plum trees will be bone,
grown delicate with frost's
formalities. Their black
angles will tear the snow.

Death of a Cat

His nightmare rocked the house
but no one woke, accustomed
to the heart's disturbances.

We dug a grave last night
under the apple tree where fruit
fattens in green clusters.

Black and white fur perfect
except where soil fell
or where small blood seeped

between the needles of her teeth
in the cracked china of her bones.
Perfect but for darkness

clotting the skull and silence
like the note of an organ
hanging in the locked air.

Dylan dreamed it again,
woken by caterwauling.
Two mourners held a wake

at dawn on the compost heap
(her special place) yowling
to wake the sleeping and to stop

the heart, considering
animal mysteries,
the otherness of pain.

He watched, from the window,
the dawn moon dissolving
its wafer on the tongue.

Cardiff Elms

Until this summer
through the open roof of the car
their lace was light as rain
against the burning sun.
On a rose-coloured road
they laid their inks,
knew exactly, in the seed,
where in the sky they would reach
precise parameters.

Traffic-jammed under a square
of perfect blue I thirst
for their lake's fingering
shadow, trunk by trunk arching
a cloister between the parks
and pillars of a civic architecture,
older and taller than all of it.

Heat is a salt encrustation.
Walls square up to the sky
without the company of leaves
on the town life of birds.
At the roadside this enormous
firewood, elmwood, the start
of some terrible undoing.

Sheila na Gig at Kilpeck

Pain's a cup of honey in the pelvis.
She burns in the long, hot afternoon, stone
among the monstrous nursery faces
circling Kilpeck church. Those things we notice
as we labour distantly revolve
outside her perpetual calendar.
Men in the fields. Loads following the lanes,
strands of yellow hair caught in the hedges.

The afternoon turns round us.
The beat of the heart a great tongue in its bell,
a swell between bone cliffs; restlessness
that sets me walking; that second sight
of shadows crossing cornfields. We share
premonitions, are governed by moons
and novenas, sisters cooling our wrists
in the stump of a Celtic water stoop.

Not lust but long labouring
absorbs her, mother of the ripening
barley that swells and frets at its walls.
Somewhere far away the Severn presses,
alert at flood-tide. And everywhere rhythms
are turning their little gold cogs, caught
in her waterfalling energy.

Siege

I waste the sun's last hour, sitting here
at the kitchen window. Tea and a pile
of photographs to sort. Radio news
like smoke of conflagrations far away.
There isn't room for another petal
or leaf out there, this year of blossom.
Light dazzles the hedge roots underneath
the heavy shadows, burns the long grass.

I, in my father's arms in this garden
with dandelion hair. He, near forty,
unaccustomed to the restlessness
of a baby's energy. Small hands
tear apart the photograph's composure.
She pushes his chest to be let down
where daisies embroider his new shoes.

Perfumes and thorns are tearing
from the red may tree. Wild white Morello
and a weeping cherry heavy in flower.
The lilac slowly shows. Small oaks spread
their gestures. Poplars glisten. Pleated green
splits black husks of ash. Magnolia
drops its wax. Forsythia
fallen like a yellow dress.
Underfoot daisies from a deep
original root burst the darkness.

My mother, posing in a summer dress
in the corn at harvest time. Her brothers,
shadowy middle distance figures,
stoop with pitchforks to lift the sheaves.
Out of sight Captain, or Belle, head fallen
to rest in the lee of the load, patient
for the signal. Out of heart too the scare
of the field far down from the sunstruck top
of the load, and the lurch at the gate
as we ditch and sway left down the lane.

The fallen sun lies low in the bluebells.
It is nearly summer. Midges hang
in the air. A wren is singing, sweet
in a lilac tree. Thrushes hunt the lawn,
eavesdrop for stirrings in the daisy roots.
The wren repeats her message distantly,
In a race of speedwell over grass
the thrushes are silently listening.
A yellow butterfly begins
its unsteady journey over the lawn.

The radio voices break and suddenly
the garden burns, is full of barking dogs.
A woman screams and gunsmoke blossoms
in the apple trees. Sheaves of fire
are scorching the grass and in my kitchen
is a roar of floors falling, machine guns.

The wren moves closer and repeats that song
of lust and burgeoning. Never clearer
the figures standing on the lawn, sharpnesses
of a yellow butterfly, almost there.

Llŷr

Ten years old, at my first Stratford play:
The river[1] and the king[2] with their Welsh names
Bore in the darkness of a summer night
Through interval and act and interval.
Swans moves double through glossy water
Gleaming with imponderable meanings.
Was it Gielgud on that occasion?
Or ample Laughton, crazily white-gowned,
Pillowed in wheatsheaves on a wooden cart,
Who taught the significance of little words?
All. Nothing. Fond. Ingratitude. Words
To keep me scared, awake at night. That old
Man's vanity and a daughter's 'Nothing',
Ran like a nursery rhyme in my head.

Thirty years later on the cliffs of Llŷn[3]
I watch how Edgar's crows and choughs still measure
How high cliffs are, how thrown stones fall
Into history, how deeply the bruise
Spreads in the sea where the wave has broken.
The turf is stitched with tormentil and thrift,
Blue squill and bird bones, tiny shells, heartsease.
Yellowhammers sing like sparks in the gorse.
The landscape's marked with figures of old men:
The bearded sea; thin-boned, wind-bent trees;
Shepherd and labourer and night-fisherman.
Here and there among the crumbling farms
Are lit kitchen windows on distant hills,
And guilty daughters longing to be gone.

Night falls on Llŷn, on forefathers,
Old Celtic kings and the more recent dead,
Those we are still guilty about, flowers
Fade in jam jars on their graves; renewed
Refusals are heavy on our minds.
My head is full of sound, remembered speech,

---

[1]   Avon/afon: river (Welsh)   [2] Llŷr: Lear
[3]   Llŷn: N.W. Peninsula of Wales

Syllables, ideas just out of reach;
The close, looped sound of curlew and the far
Subsidiary roar, cadences shaped
By the long coast of the peninsula,
The continuous pentameter of the sea.
When I was ten a fool and a king sang
Rhymes about sorrow, and there I heard
That nothing is until it has a word.

Blodeuwedd [1]

Hours too soon a barn owl
broke from woodshadow.
Her white face rose
out of darkness
in a buttercup field.

Colourless and soundless, feathers
cream as meadowsweet
and oakflowers, condemned
to the night, to lie alone
with her sin.

Deprived too of afternoons
in the comfortable sisterhood
of women moving in kitchens
among cups, cloths and running
water while they talk,

as we three talk tonight
in Hendre, the journey over.
We pare and measure and stir,
heap washed apples in a bowl, recall
the day's work, our own fidelities.

---

[1]   Blodeuwedd: the girl made of flowers, turned into an owl
as a punishment (*The Mabinogion*)

Her night lament
beyond conversation,
the owl follows
her shadow like a cross
over the fields,

Blodeuwedd's ballad
where the long reach
of the peninsula
is black in a sea
aghast with gazing.

Shadows in Llanbadarn

All shadows on the wall are blue.
Ladder-shadow. The rope askew
on the tenth rung. The Manx kitten
leaping the gap to the orchard wall.
Yours, searching the February soil
for points of green. Papery brown
flowers of dead hydrangea stir.

From the wall to the tenth rung
the kitten drops and settles, fur
black and tiger-barred with black,
tense at the rope a breath scares.
In her face the sudden sticky green
of buds in darkness burns with sun.
Your shadow turns. I hear it on the stair.

The ladder's last. The falling sun
gradually drowns it, rung by rung.

The Water-Diviner

His fingers tell water like prayer.
He hears its voice in the silence
through fifty feet of rock
on an afternoon dumb with drought.

Under an old tin bath, a stone,
an upturned can, his copper pipe
glints with discovery. We dip our hose
deep into the dark, sucking its dryness,

till suddenly the water answers,
not the little sound we know,
but a thorough bass too deep
for the naked ear, shouts through the hose

a word we could not say, or spell, or remember,
something like 'dŵr . . . dŵr'[1].

---

[1]   Dŵr: water (Welsh)

from

Selected Poems

(uncollected elsewhere)

Syphoning the Spring

We have struggled all day to syphon water.

This morning, the air blue and the damp,
the wet, the glitter of water rose
through our fingers from a hose
dipped into drilled rock.
But the hose isn't long enough nor the hill
steep enough for water to come.
For an hour it falters in the bed of the stream
among wild forgetmenots, tracing water-veins
with their hint of mist, of water-breath.
Then we bind the pump to the hose again
and pump and pump till the bubble of rubber fills
with certain water, then drive the handle down.

Through flared fingers the water comes
like birth-water, catching green light
of fern and cresses and blue forgetmenots.

While we are sleeping
water moves in moonlight,
a slow pulse in the shallows.
Some time in the night it will stop,
in the dead hour when people die,
till we borrow more hose, find a steeper hill
so that it dares to fall clear, for it wants
to fall, to give itself, knowing the risk.

A Dream of Horses

I dreamed a gallop across sand
in and out the scallop of the tide
on a colourless horse as cold as a seal.

My hair and the mane of the horse
are the long white manes of the sea.
Every breath is a gulp of salt.

Now we are ocean. His hoof-prints
are pools, his quivering skin
the silk in the trough of the wave.

His muscular ellipses are
the sinuous long water of the sea
and I swim with the waves in my arms.

October

Wind in the poplars and a broken branch,
a dead arm in the bright trees. Five poplars
tremble gradually to gold. The stone face
of the lion darkens in a sharp shower,
his dreadlocks of lobelia grown long,
tangled, more brown now than blue-eyed.

My friend dead and the graveyard at Orcop –
her short ride to the hawthorn hedge, lighter
than hare-bones on men's shoulders, our faces
stony, rain, weeping in the air. The grave
deep as a well takes the earth's thud, the slow
fall of flowers.

                Over the page the pen
runs faster than wind's white steps over grass.
For a while health feels like pain. Then panic
running the fields, the grass, the racing leaves
ahead of light, holding that robin's eye
in the laurel, hydrangeas' faded green.
I must write like the wind, year after year
passing my death-day, winning ground.

Climbing Cader Idris

(for a mountaineer)

You know the mountain with your body,
I with my mind, I suppose.
Each, in our way, describes
the steepening angle of rock.

What difference now as we,
falling into step and conversation,
put to the test our long
thigh muscles and our breath,

turning together to the open view,
a distant plough, a lozenge of field.
We face the slope again, our boots
rough-riding the scree up, up. . . .

. . . .past the last ruined hafod[1], the last flower,
stream falling among boulders,
the mountain ewe and her lamb and at last
Llyn Cau[2] like a secret cupped in hands.

You climb on to the summit
'to test my body further'.
I prefer to stare at shirred water
and the vast face of stone.

I search for words.
While I'm still catching my breath
you describe that dizzy joy
at the sheer page,

'A move so delicate
along a traverse,
just fingertip
between the hold and the fall'.

---

[1]   hafod: a shepherd's summer house
[2]   Llyn Cau: a lake under Cader Idris mountain

Castell y Bere[1]

So many deaths under unfurling trees
or on banks where primrose makes us dizzy
after ten miles of mountain track –

a lamb's head clean as a toy, the beads
of its vertebrae picked smooth as hail maries,
hobby horse, head on a stake, Llywelyn
shorn of his coat to mother-smell an orphan
for the grieving ewe.

In the barn that other lamb
a husk in my hands, delicate and swift
as a chalk horse, its four hooves galloping
no-where forever in its attitude
of birth, stillborn on its journey, still
in the caul of its skin, not skeleton
but bas-relief, little sea-horse, womb-horse.

In the wood the jay's discarded robe,
barred-blue wing-feathers, fallen black arrows
of flight, breast-down cream, rose, terra cotta,
a quiver of feathers, a drop of fresh blood
in calm afternoon but no bird at all.

Then the kestrel on its back in torchlight
dead with Tonfannau's[2] ghostly soldiery
in the deserted military camp.
On a concrete floor littered with glass
and owl-pellets, his royal feathers dressed
impeccably black and gold as heraldry.
His turned head is a skull, his breast
a seethe of hatching spiders.

---

[1]   Castell y Bere: the name of one of Prince Llewelyn's castles
[2]   Tonfannau: site of a World War II British training camp

Today

Kate in full day in the heat of the sun
looks into the grave, sees in that unearthing
of a Roman settlement, under a stone
only the shadow of a skeleton.

Gwyn on his back in the dark, lying
on the lawn dry from months of drought,
finds in the sky through the telescope
the fuzzy dust of stars he had been searching.

Imprint of bones is a constellation
shining against silence, against darkness,
and stars are the pearly vertebrae
of water-drops against the drought, pelvis,

skull, scapula five million light years old
wink in the glass, and stardust is all we hold
of the Roman lady's negative
in the infinite dark of the grave.

Taid's Grave

Rain on lilac leaves. In the dusk
they show me the grave,
a casket of stars underfoot,
his name there, and his language.

Voice of thrushes in rain.
My cousin Gwynfor eases me
into the green cave.
Wet hands of lilac

touch my wrist and the secret
unfreckled underside of my arm
daring fingers to count
five warm blue eggs.

Tadzekistan

From the little plane
to Samarkand, rickety as a toy,
through gauzy heat a green geometry
glitters with miraculous white roses
of water on their silver conduits.

The image jumps
like old film under the rattling wing.
The desert, not gold as in children's books,
but mountainous and grey with stone-dust,
the cotton-fields laid out like carpets,

prayer rugs in the drought.
Walking, later, in the hot ash
of the ancient desert city, I see
the impossible silver battlements
of distant glaciers, and in the valley

water's quicksilver,
its Catherine wheels, its memory
of fern-designs that lean in wet places,
of feathers dropping from water-birds,
of dizzy vortices that know the way to spin.

It is a melted mountain
come so far in the dark pipes and channels.
Yet it learns again the colour of the ice
it was. From here we look from the precipice,
hear a dog bark, a child cry, a cockerel crow,

see a Tadzek woman hang
clean cotton in the sun like any wife.
Let us praise hydro-engineers and five-year plans.
Let us praise the designer of ice-mountains glittering blue
on a far horizon like a wild idea.

Shearing

No trouble finding them. Their cries
rise with the wind along the lane
spiced with hawthorn and golden chain.

A shovel turning snow, the blade
slides under the filthy fleece
to sugar-almond flesh,

turning the wool's silver, spreads it
in the dirt of the barn, whole,
wide as a double quilt.

In the orchard the ewes grieve.
Warm winds herd them, begin
to heal their nakedness.

A sheepdog with silver eyes
listens for cries and silences
under trailing electric flexes.

At tea-break we rest, the smells of wool
like wet Burberries going home from school
delayed in woods by a pool of sticklebacks,

that space between two activities
where something is lost and somebody's
footsteps are following you home.

And innocently, helping Nanna,
I pass tea to the thin, dark man
in the blue boiler-suit and move on,

take out my camera for a picture
of shearing-day, Hywel, Nanna,
and helpers from neighbouring farms.

Next day, still in my camera not smiling,
he died in a noose in his own barn
leaving Hywel his moon-eyed dog.

The wind got up and it was colder,
though wool still curded hawthorn lanes,
chaining the farms to each other.

from

Letting in the Rumour

At One Thousand Feet

Nobody comes but the postman
and the farmer with winter fodder.

A-road and motorway avoid me.
The national grid has left me out.

For power I catch wind.
In my garden clear water rises.

A wind spinning the blades
of the mill to blinding silver

lets in the rumour,
grief on the radio.

America telephones.
A postcard comes from Poland.

In the sling of its speed the comet
flowers to perihelion over the chimney.

I hold the sky to my ear to hear
pandemonium whispering.

Neighbours

That spring was late. We watched the sky
and studied charts for shouldering isobars.
Birds were late to pair. Crows drank from the lamb's eye.

Over Finland small birds fell: song-thrushes
steering north, smudged signatures on light,
migrating warblers, nightingales.

Wing-beats failed over fjords, each lung a sip of gall.
Children were warned of their dangerous beauty.
Milk was spilt in Poland. Each quarrel

the blowback from some old story,
a mouthful of bitter air from the Ukraine
brought by the wind out of its box of sorrows.

This spring a lamb sips caesium on a Welsh hill.
A child, lifting her face to drink the rain,
takes into her blood the poisoned arrow.

Now we are all neighbourly, each little town
in Europe twinned to Chernobyl, each heart
with the burnt fireman, the child on the Moscow train.

In the democracy of the virus and the toxin
we wait. We watch for bird migrations,
one bird returning with green in its voice,

glasnost
golau glas,[1]
a first break of blue.

Windmill

On the stillest day
not enough breath to rock the hedge
it smashes the low sun to smithereens.

Quicker than branch to find a thread of air
that'll tow a gale off the Atlantic
by way of Lundy, Irish Sea.

At night it knocks stars from their perches
and casts a rhythmic beating of the moon
into my room in bright blades.

---

[1]   golau glas: blue light

It kneels into the wind-race
and slaps black air to foam.
Helping to lower and lift it again

I feel it thrash in dark water
drumming with winds from the Americas
to run through my fingers' circle

holding the earth's breath.

Listening for Trains

I.

All day gale-warnings
Hard to believe when air hangs

wet in the plum-trees. High
above their crowns the first sigh

touches the windmill's blades
to a blurred cloud

of wings. Then the sound
of the sea mounting the land

and the storm's engine begins.
Deep inland gardens

lap quiet as pools
under the air and nothing spills

or rustles. Out here
I'm the one with my ear

to the line,
listening for trains.

II.

Sunburnt children in baggy shorts,
Clark's sandals, cotton frocks,

gathering berries in green
backwaters through tangled vine

of woodbine, filbert and bramble.
And the day-long scramble

where the first cool touch
of hands is chance, and that brush

of another's saltiness. Underfoot
the sleepers are hot

and the parted tracks run free
until they merge above the sea

beyond the farm, the distant mill.
My heart beats against the steel

a gathering power that is mine
until I hear the train drumming the line.

Storm

The cat lies low, too scared
to cross the garden.

For two days we are bowed
by a whiplash of hurricane.

The hill's a wind-harp.
Our bones are flutes of ice.

The heart drums in its small room
and the river rattles its pebbles.

Thistlefields are comb and paper
whisperings of syllable and bone

till no word's left
but thud and rumble of

something with hooves or wheels,
something breathing too hard.

Seal

When the milk-arrow stabs she comes
water-fluent down the long green miles.
Her milk leaks into the sea, blue
blossoming in an opal.

The pup lies patient in his cot of stone.
They meet with cries, caress as people do.
She lies down for his suckling, lifts him
with a flipper from the sea's reach
when the tide fills his throat with salt.

This is the fourteenth day. In two days
no bitch-head will break the brilliance
listening for baby-cries.
Down in the thunder of that other country
the bulls are calling and her uterus is empty.

Alone and hungering in his fallen shawl
he'll nuzzle the Atlantic and be gone.
If that day's still his moult will lie
a gleaming ring on sand
like the noose she slips on the sea.

Ichthyosaur

at the exhibition of Dinosaurs from China

Jurassic travellers
trailing a wake of ammonites.
Vertebrae swirl in stone's currents,
the broken flotilla of a pilgrimage.
Bone-pods open their secret marrow.

Behind glass she dies, birth-giving.
Millions of years too late it can still move us,
the dolphin-flip of her spine
and the frozen baby turning its head
to the world at the last moment
as all babies do,
drowned as it learned to live.

Small obstetric tragedy,
like a lamb at a field-edge
the wrong way up or strangled at birth
by the mothering cord.
Perhaps earth heaved, slapped a burning hand
on both of them as he ducked under her lintel,
leaving only a grace of bones
eloquent as a word in stone.

Cold Knap Lake

We once watched a crowd
pull a drowned child from the lake.
Blue-lipped and dressed in water's long green silk
she lay for dead.

Then kneeling on the earth,
a heroine, her red head bowed,
her wartime cotton frock soaked,
my mother gave a stranger's child her breath.
The crowd stood silent,
drawn by the dread of it.

The child breathed, bleating
and rosy in my mother's hands.
My father took her home to a poor house
and watched her thrashed for almost drowning.

Was I there?
Or is that troubled surface something else
shadowy under the dipped fingers of willows
where satiny mud blooms in cloudiness
after the treading, heavy webs of swans
as their wings beat and whistle on the air?

All lost things lie under closing water
in that lake with the poor man's daughter.

Apples

They fill with heat, dewfall, a night of rain.
In a week they have reddened, the seed gone black
in each star-heart. Soft thud of fruit
in the deepening heat of the day.
Out of the delicate petals of secret skin
and that irreversible moment when the fruit set,
such a hard harvest, so cold and sharp on the tongue.

They look up from the grass, too many to save.
A lapful of windfalls with worms in their hearts,
under my thumb the pulse of original sin,
flesh going brown as the skin curls over my knife.
I drown them in water and wine, pushing them under,
then breathe apples simmering in sugar and spice,
fermenting under the tree in sacs of juice
so swollen they'd burst under a wasp's foot.

Oranges

So many of them among the stones,
each like a float over a lobster pot
coming in numerous as the drowned.

Up early at the Little Harbour,
we found the treasure we'd sought
all the Saturdays of childhood.
First gold brought generously
to a mean Britain. I remember
water calm as milk licking
the sand with little oily tongues.

We filled our shelves,
gathered our skirts to make sacks,
bumped uncomfortably homeward.
Crates like the smashed ribcages of sheep.
Across milky water the wreck
was languorous, her tilted deck
rolling with Atalanta's gold.

Salt at first bite, then bitter pith
and a sharp juice. My tongue searched
for the cloying concentrate I knew
or the scent the miner spoke of,
an orange broken at snap-time underground
breathed a mile away
if the wind's in the right direction.

Fires on Llŷn

At sunset we climb Uwchmymydd
to a land's end
where R.S. Thomas walks, finding
the footprint of God
warm in the shoe of the hare.

Words shape-shift to wind,
a flight of oystercatchers,
whinchat on a bush,
two cormorants fast-dipping wings
in a brilliant sea.

Over the holy sound
Enlli is dark in a ruff
of foam. Any pebble or shell
might be the knuckle-bone
or vertebra of a saint.

Three English boys throw stones.
Choughs sound alarm.
Sea-birds rise and twenty thousand saints
finger the shingle
to the sea's intonation.

Facing west, we've talked for hours
of our history,
thinking of Ireland
and the hurt cities,
gunshot on lonely farms,

praised unsectarian saints,
Enlli open
to the broken rosary
of their coracles,
praying in Latin and Welsh.

Done with cliff-talking
we turn inland, thinking
of home silently filling
with shadows, the hearth
quiet for the struck match,

our bed spread with clean sheets.
Our eyes are tired
with sun-gazing. Suddenly
we shout – the farms burn.
Through binoculars we see

distant windows curtained with flame.
The fires are real
that minute while we gasp,
begin to run, then realise
windows catch, not fire, but

the setting sun. We are struck still
without a word
in any language. See the hares run,
windows darken,
hear the sea's mumbled novenas.

Talking of Burnings in Walter Savage Landor's Smithy

The house eases awake to the tick
of clocks, water burbling
in the complexity of drains.
We make slow fires, smoke straight
as a cat's tail against larchwoods.
The Honddu plaits its waters in the rising sun.

Uphill the poet's house lies broken
in a memory of flame.
Face of a stranger in a holy window.
An abbey sacked and word on word
of a monk's patient flamboyance
gilds for a moment and is gone.

Cromwell fires the map.
Peasants come with roaring torches.
A terrorist's bomb.
Another falling wall.
Under the rubble a young girl's voice
blurs to silence as she lets go.

Through house and church and priory
of a tenanted land
the long fires burn, fronds
curling through the heartwood
of great houses, prising stone from stone
in two thousand years of burnings.

With petrol and a match
the ridge-beam goes and the roof sags
like the saddleback of a broken mare.
The displaced leave with their burden,
smoke pressed between scorched sheets,
and all the bridges down.

Border

It crumbles
where the land forgets its name
and I'm foreign in my own country.
Fallow, pasture, ploughland
ripped from the hill
beside a broken farm.

The word's exactness
slips from children's tongues.
Saints fade in the parishes.
Fields blur between the scar
of hedgerow and new road.
History forgets itself.

At the garage they're polite.
'Sorry love, no Welsh.'
At the shop I am slapped
by her hard 'What!'
They came for the beauty
but could not hear it speak.

Post Script

After judging the poetry competition

Epiphany – and burning of the poems
with clippings of the hedge we laid last week,
long loops of bramble, cherry, wild laburnum,
old summer leaves and sodden autumn smoke.

All afternoon I put them to the fire,
handfuls of poems turned to scrolls of vellum,
each a small chimney for a twist of air
then from each broken throat a gasp of flame.

The pages lapse and gild before they burn
like a First Folio lying in a chest.
There's splendour there (both spellings) dew and dawn,
love and philosophy and loss and lust.

Some of your poems had no voice at all
but sing now with a little sigh of death.
You would be glad to see the way your words
are turned to incense on the fire's breath.

Now they are famous on the hill for miles
and take the green wood by the throat in rage,
ode, elegy, sestina, vilanelle
scare as they couldn't, docile on the page.

The rotten core of mulch is torn apart
by the stoat-teeth of your verses, now alive.
Your scansion and your imagery start
a sting of sweetness in the bonfire's hive.

Each page committed. Your last poems burn.
Out with the cliché, archaism, weed.
They drift the hill and my mind's clean again.
New year and a fired language is what we need.

Marged

I think of her sometimes when I lie in bed,
falling asleep in the room I have made in the roof-space
over the old dark parlŵr where she died
alone in winter, ill and penniless.
Lighting the lamps, November afternoons,
a reading book, whisky gold in my glass.
At my type-writer tapping under stars
at my new roof-window, radio tunes
and dog for company. Or parking the car
where through the mud she called her single cow
up from the field, under the sycamore.
Or looking at the hills she looked at too.
I find her broken crocks, digging her garden.
What else do we share, but being women?

Overheard in County Sligo

I married a man from County Roscommon
and I live in the back of beyond
with a field of cows and a yard of hens
and six white geese on the pond.

At my door's a square of yellow corn
caught up by its corners and shaken,
and the road runs down through the open gate
and freedom's there for the taking.

I had thought to work on the Abbey stage
or have my name in a book,
to see my thought on the printed page,
or still the crowd with a look.

But I turn to fold the breakfast cloth
and to polish the lustre and brass,
to order and dust the tumbled rooms
and find my face in the glass.

I ought to feel I'm a happy woman
for I lie in the lap of the land,
and I married a man from County Roscommon
and I live at the back of beyond.

Shawl

Mamgu, a century old, loops coloured wool.
She can't see them now. The shawl

is in her mind. She touches colour.
Her fingers fly as bats at dusk in summer,

bringing the dark. The shawl grows over her knees
heavy as shadows lengthening under trees.

Her fingers write on air. She talks, walking
the old roads, tarmac'ed now, but in her mind

bone-white, scuffed by the boots of girls trailing
their hems in dust. She takes each bend,

each hill, gives every field its name.
Her hands cross-hatch the air. Garden and room

are gradually shadowed, her psalms'
memorial litany, a list of farms.

My Box

My box is made of golden oak,
my lover's gift to me.
He fitted hinges and a lock
of brass and a bright key.
He made it out of winter nights,
sanded and oiled and planed,
engraved inside the heavy lid
in brass, a golden tree.

In my box are twelve black books
where I have written down
how we have sanded, oiled and planed,
planted a garden, built a wall,
seen jays and goldcrests, rare red kites,
found the wild heartsease, drilled a well,
harvested apples and words and days
and planted a golden tree.

On an open shelf I keep my box.
Its key is in the lock.
I leave it there for you to read,
or them, when we are dead,
how everything is slowly made,
how slowly things made me,
a tree, a lover, words, a box,
books and a golden tree.

Falling

Soft slip of the loft-ladder's feet
on worn carpet. It went
under my foot on the first step
as land shelving from the littoral to the deep.

I can swim, and for a moment,
elbows on the beam over the kitchen,
I swung like a toy on a table-edge, thinking
he would catch me, free-falling.

Time slowed
as the boat of the room capsized
and I fell
till the stone floor slammed –

– while he had time
for the heart's crash and bones' brokenness,
the body like a bowl in pieces,
silence lengthening after me simple as linen.

Falling's a trust game. Fall simply
like a baby, nothing breaks.
He soothes my bruises with ointments,
brings grapes in a brown bag, his eyes

loving and sorry at the open door.
At night the soft slip of the loft-ladder
wakes me and I weep.
'You're safe now' he says, 'Sleep.'

I drop through darkness to be slammed awake
and always he is there, with healing.

Roadblock

Over and over these nights I dream of horses.
Sometimes I'm walking the known lane home
to find them standing, immovable giants
blocking my way. No creak of brass or harness.
No stamping hoof. Bronze beasts in a museum,
gold flanks flowing in a still compliance,
each head curved over another's neck,
and past the mass of them the house-lights gleaming.
I remember beautiful boys on the road from school
shouldering courage between them, beast in check
but only just, and my heart beating
too fast for love and fear of them. In the cool
dawn I'm stark awake. You're dead to the world
blocking my way to somewhere with your sleeping gold.

Binary

for Owain

You take blue plums from a bowl
'Think only of two. Each answer's yes or no.'

Negative. Positive. Light flickers in my mind
coming and going in uncertainty,
doubt's dark nebula against a galaxy.

In old films held to light
you are new-born, small child,
and we count fingers and toes.
The little pig squeals all the way home.
We count stairs to ease the way to bed,
trees, gates, lamp-posts on a long walk.

The bloom of blue plums holds your fingerprint.
'You do it now. Each plum is two.'

It should be easier than fingers.
Pairs mean more. Couples. Parents.
Mother and child. The body's symmetry.
I move a plum, think multiples of two.
I have it. The answer's right.
You're pleased with both of us.

In the cold sky I show you Jupiter,
its Galilean moons, the nebula
that rears its head before Orion's sword,
and Algol, blue dwarf and yellow giant
true binary star that calculates the dark
and counts its little day in the wink of an eye.

You teach me binary and distant coda
deep in the dark tracks of songs you make,
uncountable chords like Saturn's echoing rings.
I listen, counting sound,
wild poetry you sing to your guitar.
Your brother drums.
I think I understand.

The Hare

i.m. Frances Horovitz 1938-1983

That March night I remember how we heard
a baby crying in a neighbouring room
but found him sleeping quietly in his cot.

The others went to bed and we sat late
talking of children and the men we loved.
You thought you'd like another child. 'Too late.'

you said. And we fell silent, thought a while
of yours with his copper hair and mine,
a grown daughter and sons.

Then, that joke we shared, our phases of the moon.
'Sisterly lunacy' I said. You liked
the phrase. It became ours. Different

as earth and air, yet in one trace that week
we towed the calends like boats reining
the oceans of the world at the full moon.

Suddenly from the fields we heard again
a baby cry, and standing at the door
listened for minutes, eyes and ears soon used

to the night. It was cold. In the east
the river made a breath of shining sound.
The cattle in the field were shadow black.

A cow coughed. Some slept, and some pulled grass.
I could smell blossom from the blackthorn
and see their thorny crowns against the sky.

And then again, a sharp cry from the hill.
'A hare' we said together, not speaking
of fox or trap that held it in a lock

of terrible darkness. Both admitted
next day to lying guilty hours awake
at the crying of the hare. You told me

of sleeping at last in the jaws of a bad dream.
'I saw all the suffering of the world
in a single moment. Then I heard

a voice say "But this is nothing, nothing
to the mental pain".' I couldn't speak of it.
I thought about your dream as you lay ill.

In the last heavy nights before full moon,
when its face seems sorrowful and broken,
I look through binoculars. Its seas flower

like cloud over water, it wears its craters
like silver rings. Even in dying you
menstruated as a woman in health

considering to have a child or no.
When they hand me insults or little hurts
and I'm on fire with my arguments

at your great distance you can calm me still.
Your dream, my sleeplessness, the cattle
asleep under a full moon,

and out there
the dumb and stiffening body of the hare.

Hare in July

All spring and summer the bitch has courted the hare,
thrilled to the scent in a gateway, the musk of speed.
Months while I dug and planted and watched a mist
of green grow to a dense foliage,
neat rows in a scaffolding of sticks and nets,
nose down, tail up in thickening grass
she has been hunting the hare.

Today the big machines are in the field
raising their cromlechs against the sun.
The garden is glamorous with summer.
We cut and rake grass for the fire.
She leaps the bank bearing the weight of her gift,
the golden body of a young jack hare,
blood in its nostrils and a drowning sound.

'Drop' we say 'drop'. Heartbeat running out,
its eyes as wide and black as peaty lakes.
I feel under my finger one snapped rib
fine as a needle in a punctured lung
where it leaped too wild against the bitch's jaw.
Light fades from its fur, and in its eyes
a sudden fall of snow.

Trophy

> *'Thorpe Satchville Beagles, 3 hours,*
> *Clawson, January 26th 1928'*

In the ice-trap of January
trees splinter a low sun
and the pond's brilliance
is glazed to pearl like the eye
of the old blind dog.

Hares start from furrows
to fire the land, their ears
small standing shadows, each bone
an instrument for listening,
each foot on the pulse of the earth.

Musk in the brain, the hounds
are a parliament of braying.
Of all creatures the hare
has the largest heart,
his blood-volume the greatest.

This one outran the pack
for a hare's nine lives,
and does again through an afternoon
when trees sing in ice, and air
is opal for three winter hours.

I heard of a hare who outran hounds
for a day and died of heartburst, found
at his death-moment, his arteries
full of air-bubbles instead of blood.
Or hares on aerodrome runways racing jets.

When they cast the torn body away
and saved the golden head
for the taxidermist's shield,
in turn they emptied the horn
in The Star, Long Clawson.

At Thorpe Satchville the kennelman
set bowls before his pets,
and rubbed their coats
to their usual shining.

The Rothko Room

He crushed charcoal with a city's rubies,
saw such visions of soft-edged night and day
as stop the ears with silence. In this,
the last room after hours in the gallery,
a mesh diffuses London's light and sound.
The Indian keeper nods to sleep, marooned
in a trapezium of black on red.

We few who stop are quiet as if we prayed
in this room after Turner's turbulence.
Coming and going through paint's water-curtains
turning a corner suddenly we find
a city burns, a cathedral comes down
with a last blaze filling its gaudy lantern
and windows buckle as a tenement falls.

Rack the heart for memory or sense
and reds like these come crowding out of dream:
musk mallow, goat's rue, impatiens,
loosestrife, hellebore, belladonna, nightshade,
poppysilks crushed in their velvety soot,
and digitalis purpurea, red on maroon,
drop dappled gloves along an August lane.

A morning's laundry marking glass with steam
on rainy Mondays where a blackbird sings
sodden in dripping dark-red lilac trees.
We look, myopic, down his corridors
through misted spectacles of broken glass
window on window, scaffolding of pain
red on maroon and black, black on maroon.

Red Poppy

from a painting by Georgia O'Keefe

'The meaning of a word
is not as exact
as the meaning of a colour'

So she walks out of the rectangles
of hard, crowded America
and floods the skies over southern plains

with carmine, scarlet,
with the swirl of poppy-silk.
There is music in it, and drumbeat.

You can put out the sun with poppy,
lie in long grass with beetle and ladybird
and shade your eyes with its awnings,

its heart of charcoal.
Wine glasses held to candles
or your veined lids against the sun.

The waters open for a million years,
petal after petal in the thundering river,
stamens of flying spray at its whirlpool heart.

Red mountain where the light slides
through the beating red of every Texan dusk,
and dark earth opens in a sooty yawn.

She paints out language, land, sky,
so we can only look and drown in deeps
of poppy under a thundering sun.

February

Lamb-grief in the fields
and a cold as hard as slate.
Foot and hoof are shod

with ice. Our footprints
seem as old as ferns in stone.
Air rings in ash and thorn.

Ice on the rain-butt, thick
as a shield and the tap chokes,
its thumb in its throat.

The stream runs black
in a ruff of ice, its caught breath
furls a frieze of air.

At night ice sings
to the strum of my thrown stones
like a snapped harp-string.

The pond's glass eye holds
leaf, reed, fish, paperweight
in a dream of stone

Gannet

hangs on the wind on motionless wings
and falls a hundred feet

on a gleam of fish.
The sea gasps

as the hiss of iron
in the farrier's bucket.

The black wave,
a white-hot knife of light,

sea's retina dazzled
by the sign of the cross.

Night Flying

We fall to earth like children playing war.
Low-flying jets by night,
their roar out of dark breaks sleep.
Attack comes from behind, blindfolding us.
It's not like playing but remembering war,
crouching under the stairs for the all-clear.

They see through our uncurtained windows
as we turn to each other in the dark.
They search the fields with their night eye
for creatures crossing no-man's-land,
a sniper on a branch, a hare
with the moon in its eye, a terrorist
taking the ditch way home, white faces
at windows of lonely farms.

Who knows what outrages we'd be plotting
in bedroom and burrow and hollow oak,
what subterfuge we'd be dreaming, what outbreak
of peace, what tender subversions as we cry
in each other's arms at such an outrage
as their shadows cross the moonlit garden,
quartering the privacy of dreams.

In January

A day of wings – jet from Aberporth,
glittering dragonfly
towing its shadow from the south
over a yellow hill. It breaks the day.

Ice beneath the dog's paw cries
in the silence we're left with. A pair
of buzzards circle in bright air
slowly over an oakwood, and three crows

come up for air from a frozen field.
Over the brow, where the lane falls
into sheer light, air is filled
with clouds of glassy insect wings.

The cities can forget on days like this
all the world's wars. It's we
out on the open hill who see
the day crack under the shadow of the cross.

Tory Party Conference, Bournemouth, 1986

for Bill Davies

While Bill was dancing on his window-sill
to a song called 'Up on the Roof'
the police were mounting the stairs.

He rocked the town with his eye,
tilted the streets and rooftops,
rolling the warships in the Channel.

Da Vinci's proportioned man
his limbs outreaching
for the perfect circle.

The town trembled in the glass
as he pirouetted on his little stage
till the police broke down the door.

Then he learned how for minutes he'd danced
in the sights of the marksman's gun,
his fingers and feet describing

the cold ring of its eye.

Times like These

Too heavy-hearted to go walking
in beech-woods. At night the children's sleep
is racked by dreams. They wake crying of war.
Pushing a pram in 1961,
I remember how love weighed, anger shored
against helplessness, how we wrote letters
to the papers, raged at Strontium 90,
the bitter rain that stained our mother-milk.

Yet my daughter's beautiful,
and my daughter's daughter, even then printed
in the womb of the waking embryo,
now resolves into her elements.
Shadow on shining, here she comes dancing
through the bright window of ultra-sound,
fiercer than death and kicking to be born.

In times like these we should praise trees and babies
and take the children walking in beech-woods.

Slate Mine

Into the dark out of June heat,
under the forest's root, past Private,
Danger, Forbidden, past wheels, pulleys,
chains stilled in their pollens of rust.

We stoop through its porch,
to the knees in ice. Torchlight flutters
on wet stone and dies at the brink
of the first gallery.

In the next, and the next, emptiness deep
as cathedrals, then one where a stream hangs
three hundred feet in glittering stillness
and ferns lean to drink at sunlight.

Rungs crook rusted fingers over the drop,
the miner's footprint in air, his hand-print
on rockface and roofscape slimed
by a century of rain.

My cast slate panics
through generations of silence,
such a long wait
for the sound of drowning.

Roofing

Is it the regularity of slate
or thought of the body safe in its den
that makes the raising of the roof so right?

Somewhere for drumming knucklebones of rain
in the rattled nervousness of night,
or shawls of January snow thrown

over a domestic geometry.
Last day of the year. The hammer taps,
setting the courses against winter sky.

Neat as a darn they lap and overlap.
With frozen hands we put the tools away.
The afternoon has lapsed. Dusk mends the gap

with slate-dark purples, and where the holes are
the risen wind comes in, and the first star.

Hearthstone

Lifting the slab takes our breath away
Corner to edge, edge to corner.
Its weight steps the plank
shifting from foot to foot.

The van groans slowly home.
We pause to think, eye the gap
and heave again.
A quarter of a ton.

What weighs is the power of it
trembling at finger-tip,
its balancing moment
held like feathers.

Grindings pressed to slate
electric in my hands. We lean
on the ropes and let it
slowly into fresh cement.

Its purples multiplied
as snows, rains, rivers
that laid themselves down
too finely to see or count,

as many stone-years as wings
of the heath blue, jay feather, layers
of oak-shadow, beechmast,
print of a mountain-ash on rockface.

The tree in the crevice, quarryman
in the glittering slip of rain
on million-faceted blue Blaenau,
the purples of Penrhyn.

So the dairy slab that cooled
junkets and wheys, wide dishes of milk
beading with cream, skims for churning,
now becomes pentanfaen,

hearthstone. Milky planets
trapped in its sheets
when the book was printed,
float in the slate,

water-marked pages
under a stove's feet.

Pipistrelle

Dusk unwinds its spool
among the stems of plum-trees,
subliminal messenger
on the screen of evening,
a night-glance as day cools
on the house-walls.

We love what we can't see,
illegible freehand
fills every inch of the page.
We sit after midnight
till the ashes cool
and the bottle's empty.

This one, in a box, mouse
the size of my thumb in its furs
and sepia webs of silk
a small foreboding,
the psalms of its veins
on bible-paper,

like a rose I spread once in a book
till you could read your future
in the fine print.

Fulmarus Glacialis

for Christine Evans

Filing the fulmar you post me from Llŷn
I turn to the bird-book and the cliffs.

Found first in Iceland, 1750,
glacial bird whose wings of snow
throw images of angels on the sea
or a gutfull of stinking oil in the enemy's face.

Pilgrim. Discoverer. On the bird-map
Britain's little island's coiffed
with foam of fulmar.
Once rare visitor, she takes the coast.

Between small-print of shore
and broad stroke of the littoral
is fulmar territory, Rockall to Fastnet,
Lundy to Hebrides.

In seabird's slow increase she drew the map
in feathery sea-script, set her single egg
on the palm of every ledge
till that first visitor became a million birds.

Bridle the fulmar. Borrow the lover's llatai[1]
for carrying a message to a friend
a hundred miles or so across the Bay
down the bright water-lines, Ceredigion to Llŷn.

Racing Pigeon

Sunburst of angel
from the dark of a thornbush.
The spaniel makes a dash for it
and has to be held back.

It struts in its anklets
ruffling on the high wall,
storm-blown from the sea,
charts erased from its brain.

---

[1] llatai: a bird is used as a lover's messenger in
Medieval Welsh poetry

It suns itself on warm stone
and takes our hospitality,
a dish of sunflower seeds,
a bowl of rainwater.

Day after day it inclines less
to the lost road of the air,
tries a small circle on blue,
cannot find the thread of wind that brought it.

Somewhere the track ran out under its wings.
There's something we try to remember,
like conscience
at the edge of the mind.

I try again to read its bracelets
but before I'm sure it turns
on rose-quartz toes,
its eye a ring of fire.

Sun runs a finger
over its collar of opals.
Wind stirs the cirrus of its throat,
taking its time.

Magpie in Snow

Etched where it flew
under the garden table, twice
breasting the drift, spread feathers
of flight cut in the snow's glass,

two fingerprints
in Leonardo's sketchbooks
where grain and force of waves
are held in ice. Magpies

skim snow at the speed of hunger
and snow like memory or rock
remembers. Here's the whirr
of wings in your ear and a sob

of frozen air. At daybreak
while we slept it left its image
in the mirror, filled the shallows
with a rinse of palest blue.

Tawny Owl

Plainsong of owl
moonlight between cruciform
shadows of hunting.

She sings again
closer
in the sycamore,

her coming quieter
than the wash
behind the wave,

her absence darker
than privacy
in the leaves' tabernacle.

Compline. Vigil.
Stations of the dark.
A flame floats on oil

in her amber eye.
Shoulderless shadow
nightwatching.

Kyrie. Kyrie.

Peregrine Falcon

New blood in the killing-ground,
her scullery,
her boneyard.

I touch the raw wire
of vertigo
feet from the edge.

Her house is air. She comes downstairs
on a turn of wind.
This is her table.

She is arrow.
At two miles a minute
the pigeon bursts like a city.

While we turned our backs
she wasted nothing
but a rose-ringed foot

still warm.

Clocks

for Cai

We walk the lanes to pick them.
'Ffwff-ffwffs'. He gives them the name
he gives to all flowers. 'Ffwff! Ffwff!'
I teach him to tell the time
by dandelion. 'One o' clock. Two.'
He blows me a field of gold
from the palm of his hand
and learns the power of naming.

The sun goes down in the sea
and the moon's translucent.
He's wary of waves and sand's
soft treachery underfoot.
'What does the sea say?' I ask.
'Ffwff! Ffwff!' he answers, then turns
his face to the sky and points
to the full-blown moon.

Cofiant

Cofiant means biography. In Wales the tradition of
the *Cofiant* developed in the nineteenth century
when many hundreds were written, mainly about
preachers. They usually included an account of the
subject's life, a selection of his sermons, letters and
other writings and ended with tributes and an elegy.

In this poem I refer to *Cofiant a Phregethau y
Parch. Thomas Williams, Llangynog*. It was written
by his eldest son, and the eldest of his nineteen chil-
dren, my father's namesake, John Penri Williams,
and was printed in 1887. Thomas Williams was my
great-great-grandfather.

Quotations from the above *Cofiant* and from the
Chronicles of the Princes are translated from Welsh.
I refer also to *The Genealogies of Gwynedd* by J.E.
Griffith.

Houses we've lived in
inhabit us
and history's restless
in the rooms of the mind.

*

We took a flat in the family house.
Years later the old neighbour opposite
owned that, watching our arrival, she had said
'Children have come to live at Number One.'

The rooms were tall and hollow. Sun
printed the boards with parallelograms.
Between stained borders floors showed ghosts
of carpets that belonged to someone else.

Nothing had changed since 1926.
'First house on the meadow', a neighbour said.
'Pheasants used to perch there on your gate.'
My widowed grandmother and her daughters

refugees who'd happened to escape
the hungry farms they'd left. Her son
had gone to sea, the desolation
of the coal-fields missed by chance.

*

We came in March and month by month eight windows
that began with rain filled up with aspen leaves
as April became May and nothing was
but bluebells filling rooms with scent of blue.

*

How can you leave a house?
Do they know, who live there,
how I tread the loose tile in the hall,
feel for the light the wrong side of the door,
add my prints to their prints to my old prints
on the finger-plate?

How, at this very second,
I am crossing the room?

*

Apart from one lit, introspective square,
seventeen black windows watch the rain.
Three chimneys swallow the wind.
In the green room the gas fire wavers
as the wind breathes in.

In the brown room the piano is silent.
In another the sockets are emptied
of deck, amplifier, keyboard, guitar.
Blue-tack pegs the empty poster squares
as pegs left out to green on the garden line.
There are no damp towels on the carpet,
no paint drying or gaudy disorder
or books folded back for reading.

The front door shifts in its frame.
No-one slams it. The last bus comes and goes.

Two sons were born in this bed,
their sister asleep in a neighbouring room.
Dam-burst in the pit of the pelvis,
belly-blow of sea in a hidden cave.
The blaze whitened my mind,
my heart clenched its fist of blood.
No wonder they speak of stars
and storms in heaven.

*

'And it was the six hundred and ninetieth year of Christ.
And the milk and butter were changed to blood.
And the moon changed to the colour of blood.'

*

Blaen Cwrt, longhouse,
stepping-stone for the west wind's foot.
Colby, called Number One
with its pebble-dash symmetry.
Ship-shaped Flatholm of the island name.
Bryn Isaf on the hill
above the weed-blurred railway line.
Ceryg-yr-Wyn where the clergyman's
nineteen children were born.
A new Cae Coch on the crossroads
beside the ruined birthplace.
Crugan, four-square farm in slate and stone
in acres of good land.
Bachellyn derelict, where the brother lived.
Broom Hall, the rich son's house of treasure
with Werglodd Fawr in ruins under its feet.
Hendrewen and Chwilog, old lost farms
and nameless hovels, halls and castles
of the far-off dead long fallen to ruin.

*

Gruffydd (1047)

'And then about seven-score men
of Gruffydd's tribe
died through the treachery
of the men of Ystrad Tywi.
And to avenge his men
Gruffydd ravaged Dyfed and Ystrad Tywi.
And there came a great snow
on the Calends of January
and it lasted until the Feast of Patrick.'

*

Wind felled the poplar
with an axe of air.

Its roots tilted a shield
of fibrous mould.

All day we worked in the cold sun,
bill-hook, chainsaw and axe crossing the grain.

Broken ripples, annular rings
counting the generations.

*

Their midsummer wedding
a year before my birth.
Wasn't I there, in the June heat?
I call back breath of roses,
fields of cut hay over a chapel wall.
A perfect day for harvest.
My mother's brothers itch in borrowed clothes
sniffing the air for rain,
running a finger underneath stiff collars.
Black curls spring from combed water,
eyes clear as summer
under the thunder of the brows.

A festival in my mind
or funeral I have mixed with roses
in the album's tinted photographs.

*

John Penri Williams (1899-1957)

In the margins of books, poems printed
on foxed, bevelled pages; under the shelf
where we peeled back the old wallpaper;
lists; old letters; diaries; notebooks;
copperplate in blacklead and washable Quink,
the Conway Stewart with a golden lever
and its intake of sound as the ink-sac swelled;
commentary; schedules; signatures.
How, after thirty years, do I know his hand?

Chapel boy from Carmarthenshire
locked in his cabin, writing home,
'Annwyl Mam,' shocked by crew-talk,
or tapping morse as the world burned.
He drummed bad news on the sea's skin,
his air-waves singing over the roof
of the whale's auditorium. Only his heart,
the coded pulse over dark water
to a listening ship and the girl at home.

Twenty years away his daughter waits
to knock him dizzy with her birth
and scarcely twenty more
he'll strike her silent with his death,
going out on a rainy evening
in May when she isn't looking,
with a 'Hwyl fawr, Cariad.'
No message. Just, 'Over'.

*

An over-turned wine-glass
in wet grass,
one sip like guilt
in the spoon of the tongue.

The fire's dissolved
to bird-bones.
A small lake shivers
in the deck-chair's lap.

*

Phyllis (1895-1985)

Nearly ninety, leaning on my arm,
taking me down the road on her usual walk,
my aunt, his sister, stopped at the iron railings.
We looked down on the flood-plain of the Tywi
from where steep ground brought the town to a sudden halt.
Old settlements, broken things showing their bones,
the Roman 'caer' branded on the town's name,
the medieval church, the Civil War,
and down there the unmistakable straight line
between trees and scrub and bramble hedges:
'The Aberystwyth train', she said, seeing a puff
of steam, hearing the shunt of its struggle
out of the distant station.

All the way to the sea
you can still see where it went
over and under the roads, like someone blind
who remembers the way and steps out straight
through a creeping cataract of moss and bramble.

Now that she's dead when I recall her voice
she is musing to herself, 'the Aberystwyth train'.

*

Wil Williams (1861-1910)

He kept a garden
like other railwaymen
in that old world of the Great Western.
When his daughter went back
It disappointed her.
How sad, she said,
to see my mother's house so shabby,
the yard-hens scraggy,
the stackyard sour with old hay,
the house dirty.

I can't see the house in her mind,
only the white farm on the hill
that is still there.
Down through the tunnels along the line
they run away from us,
the rooms, the women who tended them,
the dressers of glinting jugs,
the lines of sweet washing between trees.
The stations with their cabbage-patches
and tubbed geraniums are closed
and the trains' long cries are swallowed
in the throats of tunnels.

*

Orchis Mascula

Hot stink of orchid in the woods at Fforest.
Downstream of the waterfall I breathed
their scent and touched their purple towers,
the swollen root that cures the King's Evil
and makes the heart hot. Not flowers to share
to bring home for a jar.
Ophelia's long purples, tragic flowers.
You could believe they grew beneath the cross
and no amount of rain could wash the blood
from their stained leaves.

They called and called but I would not hear,
mixing their voices with waves and water.
Crouched in the blackthorn tunnel the cattle made
as they swayed their way to the sea, loosed
from the beudy by Gwilym and slapped free,
I was hooked on dens and secret places,
illicit books, visions and diaries
and the tomcat stink of orchids. Nothing
would fetch me out but hunger, or the sound
of shadows stepping closer.

*

Annie (1868-1944)

I called her Ga, and a child's stuttered
syllable became her name.
A widow nearly forty years,
beautiful and straight-backed,
always with a bit of lace about her,
pearls the colour of her twisted hair,
the scent of lavender.

It was our job at Fforest to feed the hens
with cool and liquid handfuls of thrown corn.
We looked for eggs smuggled in hedge and hay,
and walked together the narrow path to the sea
calling the seals by their secret names.

At Christmas she rustled packages under her bed
where the po was kept and dusty suitcases.
That year I got an old doll with a china face,
ink-dark eyes and joints at elbows and knees.
Inside her skull, like a tea-pot, under her hair,
beneath her fontanelle, was the cold cave
where her eye-wires rocked her to sleep.

Somewhere in a high hospital window –
I drive past it sometimes with a start of loss –
her pale face made an oval in the glass
over a blue dressing-gown. She waved to me,
too far away to be certain it was her.

They wouldn't let children in.
Then she was lost or somebody gave her away.

*

First spring day in the hills.
Hens laid wild in stack and hedge.
In my palm the ice-egg
was stupidly heavy and still.

Crude pot-egg, overblown acorn
colour of bone, of fungi,
of old stone bottles,
a stone to crack a jaw.

Not delicate
like Nain's china eggs,
crazed little stone skulls,
false pregnancy, fool's gold.

Easily fooled the old hen
panicked to quicken it
under her breast-down. Stone
under the heart, stillborn.

*

Thomas Williams (1800-1885)

Child of Christmas and the turning century,
born to holy bells and the tolling sea,
he carried two voices into manhood:
the call of the sea and the call of God.

He writes how he'd never known a time
when longing for sea's rhythm
underfoot and the hot rope in his hands
reining an apron of sail as he held the wind,

was not a stinging fire in his mind,
or when the tug of religion started
turning his heart into the gale.
He took lodgings in Pwllheli and set sail.

The boat carried limestone across the Straits,
Môn to Caernarfon. He set his sights
on the torn coastline, crossing the grain
of knotty currents, westerlies and rain.

*

He was baptised in the stream at Tyddyn Shôn.
I found the place one summer afternoon
where water twisted, as it must have done,
under the bridge in a pool deep enough for a man
to drown his devils in a mountain stream,
leaving his soul caught like a rag on a stone.

*

Ceryg-yr-Wyn (1845)

'Near Christmas and the afternoon
already dark. In the yard I could hear Mary
calling the hens.

The little ones ran in and out
of the open door, their clogs
clacking on stone, till there,

a hand away on the hearth
my baby stood lifting his sleeves of fire
like a small angel of annunciation,

his laugh surprised to silence
till he fell burning into my smothering arms.
He never ran again and after three days died.

So quick the moth-wings flared
as they have done
every day since for forty years.'

*

'It was the first time grief touched my family, and I have never felt greater sorrow at the death of anyone until this day.'

*

Ceryg-yr-Wyn
3rd May 1854

Dear Son,
   Your dear mother died at 9 o'clock today and the burial has been arranged for 2 o'clock on Friday. The doctor said her main affliction was maternal tenderness, grief for Peter, and watching her other children lying sick and she unable to help them. I think Janet is a little better, but Samuel and the other children are still very ill.
      Your grieving father,
      Thomas Williams

*

Jennet (1760-1830)

Widow and widower in neighbourly grief.
She married Thomas and went to live with him
at the smallholding on the crossroads.

*

Saint Beuno's, full of breath of the sea, half
choked in elder, the wind's hymn
sings in the thorn. The monks' old

garden fends off the devil with a grove of ash.
Fruit bushes and a tangled hop-vine,
a little pasture to the lee of the wall

show how they survived against the wash
of Atlantic salt, poverty, chastity, stations
of work and prayer between sea and hill.

Where Jennet stood, to marry or mourn
three husbands or see her son baptised,
how many saints prayed on their way to die

on the holy island? How many fatherless newborn
wailed in their mothers' arms for ships capsized
in the Straits, where their fathers lie?

The church is dark for an illiterate
congregation, the lepers' window shadowed
with the living dead, those still forbidden

at our door as we cast the disconsolate
from their proper place, the sick, the doomed
who carry the virus or bacillus we call sin.

*

Under the altar a tall saint lies.
In the oval graveyard her kinsmen's bones
unthread themselves and slip among the stones

with holy relics. I can't find their grave
lost to the rampant daneberry fruited with blood
of fallen Norsemen, flourishing where they died.

*

Rowland Jones (1772-1856)
grandson of William Jones of Crugan

Brought up in Hanover Square
in a house of women,
he never married.
When he came of age
he took his fortune home.
They called him 'Mr Jones of London'.

His father burned his eyes and health with study
but the son burnished his with seeing.
He built Broom Hall among the stones
of Werglodd Fawr
and filled its rooms
with art and elegance, setting
lawns and pleasure grounds on his savage acres.

His ancestors laboured on stony farms,
thatched smallholdings, crude halls, embattled castles.
He, a gentleman, spent his life's energy
in overseeing work, a preoccupation
with plans and fine proportions.
His cousins' descendants would again

be labourers and live on smallholdings
and have their lives cut short by poverty,
taking the places of those he oversaw
building his house, setting his straight lines down,
bringing the carriage to the door to meet him
and dying of fevers that swept the poor.

*

On the twenty fourth day of February, eighteen hundred and fifty
seven, for thirteen days, Broom Hall, formerly Werglodd Fawr, in the
parish of Llanarmon in Caernarfonshire, a late Georgian house in the
austere style of the early nineteenth century, in brick stucco and slate
with slate-roofed verandahs, terraces and colonnades. House, grounds
and contents: gallery and cabinet pictures and portraits by Carracci,
Domenichino, Rubens, Teniers, Watteau, Storck, Pater, Holbein et
cetera; statuary, cabinets and tables of Florentine mosaic, ebony and
marqueterie; superb old Dresden and Oriental China; manicure sets
and silver gilt caskets, inkstands and boxes; two costly toilet cases;
valuable jewellery and filigree; eight thousand ounces of silver gilt and
silver plate; excellent household furniture; organs and musical boxes;
library of books and manuscripts; cellar of choice old wines; two hand-
some travelling carriages; phaeton, fire engine; greenhouse plants et
cetera.

*

Rowland Jones (1716-1774)
second son of William Jones of Crugan

Second son of the farm, sent to grammar school
at Botwnnog to make a lawyer of him.
Classical languages and arithmetic
were all he'd need. In a pool
of candlelight at his uncle's farm

the clever boy found wonders in his books.
Hearth-Welsh, gentry English, a scholar's Greek and Latin,
shadow-eyed in the smoke of that low room,
he found obsession on the flickering page.
Later, man of letters and law at Symond's Inn,
he studied words known since his mother's womb,
saw in old Celtic all primeval language
broken by the scattering winds of Babel
from the first stuttered monosyllable.

*

A man used to listening,
they say he overheard a confidence
and turned it to advantage.
He married money and Elizabeth,
and turned the fortune home to Eifionydd,
dreaming on Werglodd Fawr of the fine house
his infant son would build over the ruins.

*

His grave, his stone,
his parts of speech all gone
under the city's monotone.

At St James, Piccadilly,
they've tidied the torn pages
of the stones,

so there's no telling now
the body's syllables
or testament of bones.

*

Bleddyn ap Cynfyn (1069)

'And then there was the Battle of Mechain
between Bleddyn and Rhiwallon,
sons of Cynfyn,
and Meredydd and Ithel,

sons of Gruffydd.
And there the sons of Gruffydd fell.
Ithel was slain in the fight
and Meredydd perished of cold as he fled.
And there Rhiwallon ap Cynfyn was slain.
And then Bleddyn ap Cynfyn
held Gwynedd and Powys,
and Meredydd ab Owain ab Edwin
held Deheubarth.'

*

The sea wastes words
where the tide's fretwork
has worn half the hill-fort away.

It drafts and re-drafts the coast
and is never done
writing at the edge

its doodle of scum,
driftwood, rope and bottles
and skulls of birds.

*

Daughter of Penri Williams, wireless engineer of Carmarthenshire
        and Ceinwen Evans of Denbighshire
son of William Williams, railwayman and Annie of Carmarthenshire
son of Daniel Williams, railwayman of Llangynog and Sara
son of Thomas Williams, Baptist minister and Mary
son of Thomas Williams, smallholder of Nefyn and Jennet of Pystyll
son of William Williams, farmer of Crugan, Llanbedrog
son of William Jones, farmer of Crugan
son of John Williams, farmer and lawyer of Crugan
son of William and Mary
son of Robert and Margaret
son of John and Catherine
son of Robert and Elizabeth
son of Owen of Eifionydd
son of Owain
son of John

son of Meurig of Eifionydd
son of Llewelyn and Margaret Fychan
son of Cynwrig Fychan and Margaret, d. of Rhys ap Siencyn
son of Cynwrig of Llŷn and his nameless wife
son of Madog Fychan and Gwenllian, d. of Ithel Fychan
son of Madog Crupl and Margaret, d. of Rhys Fychan
son of Gruffydd, Barŵn Gwyn of Glyndyfrdwy and Margaret
son of Gruffydd, Lord of Dinas Brân and Emma Audley
son of Madog of Powys and Ysola d. of Ithel
son of Gruffydd Maelor of Powys and Angharad, d. of Owain
    Gwynedd
son of Madog of Powys and Susannah d. of Gruffydd ap Cynan
son of Meredydd of Powys and Hunydd, d. of Eunydd ap
    Gwerngwy
son of Bleddyn of Powys and Haer, d. of Cyllin ap y Blaidd Rhydd
son of Cynfyn and Angharad
son of Gwerystan and Nest
son of Gwaethfoed of Cibwr in Gwent and Morfudd, d. of Ynyr Ddu

*

from

The King of Britain's Daughter

Blood

1

The house is filled again with children.
I watch from the door, or walk,
a blue cup in my two hands,
while they dance in the drench of the grass.

The garden's a litter of gaudy, broken things,
of golden circles where the pool has been,
that little declivity below the swing
that will grass over in a week or two,

as will the scarred silence
where the hare goes
and three curlews cry.

2

Something's afoot
this summer of rain on the roof at night,
ghosts in the morning trees,
clouds thunderous with Atlantic news,

something woken where the moon
draws up her silvers from a shiver of flood
in the silted well where once
a clean spring rose,

a brim of blood I should have done with,
a forgotten dish of seed,
like the pigeon's saucer left out on the wall
when the bird had flown.

3 *Equinox*

Month of the high tides.
The small bay brims, and there,
far below us on the shore at Strumble,
not wave, not old rags,
but a seal and her newborn,
the afterbirth's ruby clean among the stones.

The children call 'Look, seal, a seal!'
We hush and look, lifting them to see
from the lighthouse wall, while far below
she rolls her slippery body in its pulse
of milk and need and afterpains
to that blind, crying mouth.

She sees us, nervous,
then lollops to the sea
to become wave, sunlight, salt,
to quicken skies and oceans
from her dish of seed,
hadlestr's1 huddle of stars.

4 *Cai*

Alert for the least sound
we'd wake to that sharp fox cry,
and find him standing in the hall,
his breath a bird in a cage.
We'd teach his heart to slow,
to let breath go under our hands and words,

as in the sun we showed him a wasp
walk free along his outstretched arm,
a caterpillar loop along his finger,
a bumble bee rescued from the house,
to hand an apple flat-palmed to a horse,
or scratch a bull's brow at the gate.

---

[1]   hadlestr: ovary (literally seed-dish, Welsh)

This time, two in the morning,
we wake suddenly to his step in the hall
and find him quiet in the lamplight
gazing at something held in his lapped hands.
Haloed and still, they don't need us,
a boy and a small stray toad in the night.

5   *Mali*

Three years ago to the hour, the day she was born,
that unmistakable brim and tug of the tide
I'd thought was over. I drove
the twenty miles of summer lanes,
my daughter cursing Sunday cars,
and the lazy swish of a dairy herd
rocking so slowly home.

Something in the event,
late summer heat overspilling into harvest,
apples reddening on heavy trees,
the lanes sweet with brambles
and our fingers purple,
then the child coming easy,
too soon, in the wrong place,

things seasonal and out of season
towed home a harvest moon.
My daughter's daughter
a day old under an umbrella on the beach
late-comer at summer's festival,
and I'm hooked again, life-sentenced.
Even the sea could not draw me from her.

This year I bake her a cake like our house,
and old trees blossom
with balloons and streamers.
We celebrate her with a cup
of cold blue ocean,
candles at twilight, and three drops of,
probably, last blood.

6

In the early dusk
rain and September bring,
we lit two candles in the conservatory.
They counted from across the table
the eight flames in our eyes,
their golden faces showed
they saw us beautiful.

What is fire? Who made the sun?
Why would it make us blind?
Above the flame, nothing
but the quiver of heat, kindling
the paper napkin you held in white hot air
to see it gild before it flew,
an angel burning in the dark.

It's all too much – the moon
cock-eyed above us through the glass,
our faces in the dangerous angel-light,
wildfire of stars.
Baths, pyjamas, poems, bed,
three struggling bodies, hearts aflame.
It ends in tears.

7 *Coyan*

The child brings a bone from the sea.
'Fish!' Old tree-thing, driftwood,
It dries for weeks on the high shelf above the Rayburn,
He watches it sometimes, 'My fish!'

In the excitement of the last day
he forgot it, a twist of water stilled
in the current. I'm sure he dreams of it.
Next year he'll tell me how he wakes, crying,

of a great fish swimming in the city streets
tossed like the cans we aimed our stones at,
a fibula of moonlight on his bedroom floor,
a taste of salt when he kissed us goodbye.

Musician

for Owain

His carpet splattered like a Jackson Pollock
with clothes, books, instruments, the *NME*,
he strummed all day, read Beethoven sonatas.
He could hear it, he said, 'like words.'

That bitterest winter, he took up the piano, obsessed,
playing Bartok in the early hours. Snow fell,
veil after veil till we lost the car in the drive.
I slept under two duvets and my grandmother's fur,
and woke, suffocating, in the luminous nights
to hear the Hungarian Dances across moonlit snow.
The street cut off, immaculate, the house
glacial, suburbs hushed in wafery whiteness.
At dawn, hearing Debussy, I'd find him,
hands in fingerless gloves against the cold,
overcoat on. He hadn't been to bed.

Snows banked the doors, rose to the sills,
silted the attic, drew veils across the windows.
Scent, sound, colour, detritus lay buried.
I dreamed the house vaulted and pillared with snow,
a drowned cathedral, waiting for the thaw,
and woke to hear the piano's muffled bells,
a first pianissimo slip of snow from the roof.

The Listeners

On SS *Hatimura*, 1919,
he wrote home
from somewhere in the Pacific.

A quiet night.
He listened for the hum of news
in his cabin of wires,
for the swell sweeping the deck,
the rising of the wind.
The signal's beam swung over the void,
voice to voice touching in circles
that could lap the world.

We listen,
cupping our instruments to space
for the rhythmic signal
that might be someone,
Mozart, Euclid,
an ordered intelligence
aeons too late to answer.

If anyone's out there listening
they'll catch the century's radio waves
swimming out forever,
a shoal of whispers rustling past the stars,
the murmured words as he wrote home,
his voice saying 'I am calling you
from SS *Hatimura*'.

Anorexic

My father's sister,
the one who died
before there was a word for it,
was fussy with her food.
'Eat up,' they'd say to me,
ladling a bowl with warning.

What I remember's
how she'd send me to the dairy,
taught me to take cream,
the standing gold.
Where the jug dipped
I saw its blue-milk skin
before the surface healed.

Breath held, tongue between teeth,
I carried in the cream,
brimmed, level,
parallel, I knew,
with that other, hidden horizon
of the earth's deep
ungleaming water-table.

And she, more often than not half-dressed,
stockings, a slip, a Chinese kimono,
would warm the cream, pour it
with crumbled melting cheese
over a delicate white cauliflower,
or field mushrooms
steaming in porcelain,

then watch us eat, relishing,
smoking her umpteenth cigarette,
glamorous, perfumed, starved,
and going to die.

The Vet

'Would the child like to leave?
It won't be pleasant.'

But I'm stuck with it,
brazening out the cowshed
and the chance of horror,
not knowing how to leave
once I'd said I'd stay.

Gloved to the elbow in blood
and her mysterious collar of muscle,
he wrenched from the deep cathedral of her belly
where her heart hung and the calf swam in its pool,
a long bellowing howl
and a rope of water.

I got off lightly that time,
no knife, no severing,
no inter-uterine butchery
to cut them free.

He let go the rope of water
and the calf swam home like a salmon
furled in a waterfall,
gleaming, silver, sweet under the tongue
of his brimming mother.

Baltic

The air is white and dense
where fishermen dip their hooks
into black silence,
and it's hard to believe in islands
half a mile away in the mist,
the delicate archipelago of the map.

Six posts step out to sea, ice-locked
where water laps in summer,
and boats waltz on their slack ropes.
Salt-smells, fish, bird-cries
locked in the sea's cellar,
the land under wraps.

You can drive to Sweden, they tell me,
or catch the post for Stockholm half way over.
Trying to believe it, I walk on the sea,
out between the posts until I'm lost in whiteness,
wondering, without a bird's talent for magnetism,
how I'll know the way.

Hölderlin in Tubingen

for Paul Hoffmann

The river remembers,
then crumples in a frown of loss:
a garden of children and laundry at the brink,
the white face of a man shut in the mind's tall tower.

In the October garden, where the carpenter's children
played between the high wall and the water,
apples fall, and fire-tongues of cherry
crackle in the grass for us to shuffle.

The great willow that the poet knew,
only half itself since the hurricane,
kneels into a current that's deeper
and more powerful than it seems.

Upstairs, in his white, three-windowed hemisphere,
where for forty years they cared for him, light
shivers on the ceiling, bird-shadows touch and go,
things that were clear break up and flow away:

his poems on the wall,
quick freehand in the visitors' book,
a jar of flowers on bare boards,
a drift of red leaves on three windowsills.

So small, his bed must have been here,
his table there for the light, and the door
where the carpenter's daughter listened for his rages
and brought him bread, meat, a bowl of milk.

The swan turns on her own reflection. Silence
is her image. Currents pull. The willow
trawls its shadow, searching for something
in the broken face of water.

The river remembers everything, its long muscle
bearing the weight of rain a month ago,
the touch of waterbirds miles upstream,
the heavy step of a waterfall in its deep subconscious,

and the white, raging pages
that once beat their foreheads
on its scattering surface
before drowning.

The Poet

We sweat the afternoon
in the muslin-light of the marquee
under the shadows of birds.
Outside, pigeons complain in the heat
to the harp's sharp fire.

Then his voice,
the first unthreading of a sea-wind,
his needle set true north
by some cold star that crackles
like a grit in the mind.

His hands are shaking, his gaze fixed
on a far shore of the spirit
beyond the flowers and the footlights.
His words cast shadows
restless as bird griefs.

Like that time once in a restaurant
when he and the Gael were talking
about song and language, he sat haloed
against a window of tropical fish
he could not see.

All the time they spoke,
I watched an angel-fish
flaunting its silks about his head,
a cold flame shaken out
of the oceans and the galaxies.

Wild Sound

for Carol Ann Duffy

A day of birds:
at dawn, my car abandoned,
engine humming at the junction,
I'm stopping the traffic, one hand up
against the hot breath of a lorry.
The other lifts the weightless silk of a swift
like a beating heart from the road.
I throw it to the wind
above the lorry and the eaves
where sky begins.

Then, in a brown underground corridor at the BBC,
an eagle owl in a hurry:
'Can't stop. On its way to Moscow.'
Then it's gone, an absence
in a wilderness,
its talons' hooked steel,
its eye planetary.

Hours later I'm still breathing
the musk of feathers. Surely
the listeners to the radio
could sense, between the words,
wild sound, hot, quivering, alive,
a wingbeat on the footless air,
a stare of gold.

Swimming with Seals

Two horizons:
a far blue line where a ship
diminishes and the evening sun
lets slip;
and submarine
where we glimpse stars and shoals
and shadowy water-gardens
of what's beyond us.

When the seal rises
she rest her chin on the sea
as we do, and tames us with her gaze.
On shore the elderly
bask beside their cars
at the edge of what they've lost,
and shade their eyes
and lift binoculars.

She's gone,
apt to the sea's grace
to watch us underwater from her place,
you with your mask and fins,
strolling the shallow gardens of the sea,
me, finding depth
with a child's flounder of limbs,
hauling downwards on our chains of breath.

For a moment the old
looking out to sea,
all earth's weight beneath their folding chairs,
see only flawless blue to the horizon,
while we in seconds of caught air,
swim down against buoyancy,
rolling in amnion
like her September calf.

Lurcher

for Dylan

Dog of Rhygyfarch and Kells
hugely pacing the room and corridor,
turns on his heels
at invisible doors.

folds himself on the Indian rug
to a gilded initial. Oiled parts
rehearse in sleep,
loosing long golden farts

to great uncoilings that amaze and wake him,
his eyes' ringed planets towing moons of ice
out of the winter of a dream
at the far edge of space.

Brain too simple for his intricate body,
the spaniel shows him how to open doors.
He waits to go, patient, hind legs up and ready,
his beautiful head still down on lion forepaws.

Unleashed he flies,
illusion, hologram, he and his ghost
writing on air, on sand, two thousand years
of milgi[1] in the gold rings of his eyes.

---

[1]   milgi: greyhound (Welsh)

Lament

For the green turtle with her pulsing burden,
in search of the breeding-ground.
For her eggs laid in their nest of sickness.

For the cormorant in his funeral silk,
the veil of iridescence on the sand,
the shadow on the sea.

For the ocean's lap with its mortal stain.
For Ahmed at the closed border.
For the soldier in his uniform of fire.

For the gunsmith and the armourer,
the boy fusilier who joined for the company,
the farmer's sons, in it for the music.

For the hook-beaked turtles,
the dugong and the dolphin,
the whale struck dumb by the missile's thunder.

For the tern, the gull and the restless wader,
the long migrations and the slow dying,
the veiled sun and the stink of anger.

For the burnt earth and the sun put out,
the scalded ocean and the blazing well.
For vengeance, and the ashes of language.

No Hands

War-planes have been at it all day long
shaking the world, strung air
humming like pianos when children bang the keys

over and over; willow warbler song
and jet planes; lads high on speed up there
in a mindless thrum; down here a brake of trees

churns to a rolling wave and there's no let
in the after-quiver along air-waves struck
by silly boys who think they strum guitars,

who skim fields like surfboards over crests
of hedges, where a tractor swims in a green wake
of grass dust tossed to dry under sun and stars:

boy scaring boy off the face of his own land,
all do and dare, and look at me, no hands.

Olwen Takes Her First Steps
on the Word Processor in Time of War[1]

Her first, tentative step into the dark
deep as the void, first stone cast into nothing.
'Is anyone there?' Then the slow waiting
for a language like her own, a spark

that tells her something's there.
She takes another step across the abyss
and listens. Ticking like trodden ice
her small words skitter the black sky with stars.

All trace of bird and fox on snowy land
deleted; the guns of winter crack the lonely screen
at start of day, and where her touch has been
snowdrops come springing from the sodden ground.

In a wake of flowers she treads the dark alone
breaking the darkest page the world has known.

---

[1]   (In mythology Olwen is the girl whose feet leave white flowers
wherever she treads, instead of footprints.)

Eclipse of the Moon

Whose shadow's that?

Who walked in the evening
at his own ghost's back?

Who trod in the circle,
left a toe-print on the frozen pond?

Who looked in the mirror
and clouded the glass?

Who snatched the white moth
in his closed fist?

Who drowned
reaching for the coin?

Advent

After the wideawake galaxies
each dawn is glass.
Leavings of the night's kill lie,
twig-bones, ice-feathers,
the ghost of starlight.

Ewes breathe silver.
The rose won't come –
stopped in her tracks.
Everything's particular:
bramble's freehand,

a leaf caught out,
the lawn's journal.
Deep down even the water-table
stiffens its linen,
and horizons pleat in a bucket.

The stars burn out
to starved birds
watching my window,
and one leaf puts up a hand
against infinite light.

The Lighthouse

In the clean house on the rock
where sleepy headlands drink the evening sea
and floors are cut to fit horizons,
the great fish-eye revolves
in a socket that floats on mercury.

Waters slide and close over the drowned,
their bones add salt to salt, grains
among the sand, cries in the gull's throat.
Ninety years the beam has loomed
the century's night.

In early times it took a man's sleeve
bursting to flame one placid afternoon,
as he dipped his arm between the stilled facets,
to learn that, if revolution ceased at sunrise,
daylight could turn its eye in on itself

and burn the heart like a collapsing star,
as a child learns fire by capturing the sun
in a magnifying glass
to make Excalibur.

On Air

Tools of my father's art: old radios
of fretted wood and bakelite.
In a sanctum of shot-silk curtained window
crystal or valve lurked in its holy light.

I turned the knob. The needle wavered on
through crackling distances, Paris, Luxembourg, Hilversum,
past the call-sign of some distant station,
a lonely lightship where infinity scrambles to a hum

the Chinese whispers of a jabbering world.
And now, by transistor and satellite we hear
Beethoven in Berlin sooner than if we were there
on air-waves the speed of light. And when the wall crumbled

we heard the first stone fall before they could.
We watch storms darken the map from the crow's nest
of the weather satellite, hear the swallow's foot
on the wind's telegraph before she comes to rest,

the sun dried to a pellet in her throat.
Still lodged at the wingfeather's bloodroot
a grain of desert sand,
and on my car a veil of strange red dust.

Wind Gauge

At first barely discernible,
a faint line drawn in graphite
on a water-marked page,
hairline crack in a bird's skull.

Then one evening to the west
where light dissolves in wind and water
another rises tall as sky
to finger prevailing westerlies.

When the swallows come home
they'll ride the tangled currents
through webs of steel where once
was a wide aisle of air.

Once they raised stones,
cromlechs, megaliths, as step by step
from winter's narrowest day
they counted home the sun.

Now they hoist masts,
steel circlets to crown a hill,
restless blades against the light
generating fire out of air.

Grave God

Egyptian circa 1100 BC

Sea-wind at the door
and the song of sand on glass.
Was it Vivaldi they played
on the wind-up gramophone,
or Beethoven's *Moonlight*
fortissimo in the rattling room?

Sunday nights, my studies done,
tea on a tray and the small coal smoking,
in my hands the gift: nine inches
high, three-thousand-year-old glass
the blue of lapis lazuli,
and the smile they taught me to see
as I turned him under the lamp.

Three old sisters, their travelling days
stowed for the dark like bottled fruit,
fragments of Asia, Africa,
archaeology of Egypt, old Etruria.

Daily they walked the dunes to the beach
to stare at the sea and turn for home
where sand drifted the sills and rooms
of the wind-filled wooden bungalow,
and marram grass crept closer every day.

Tonight, under the slow light,
he composes old Egyptian blues
against a white wall,
a glitter of sand in his eye.

The Angelus

Each note delayed by the swing of the bell,
the slow weight of the rope and a swallowing wind.
Salt air and a fog off the Channel sour with furnacite,
rain on the gate, five elms on a dusk sky.
Swiftfoot over the lawn, she left an echo in the trees,
the rope dancing under dripping leaves.

In my room were eight gold counterpanes
that slipped like water when you tried to fold them.
First night, I was alone. They drove away in the rain
after family tea at the Seabank, green Lloyd Loom
and Kunzel cakes that tasted of dust,
out-of-season and nobody talking.

My new clothes smelt of navy blue wet wool,
the bloom gone out of them. Night came black to the glass,
an oval mirror swam towards me with an open mouth.
Even their kindness and the clean cave of the bed
could not keep me from the tunnel,
the shadows in a hurry along dark corridors.

Years later I went back.
They showed me pretty rooms,
bright girls racing somewhere, preoccupied,
and across the lawn where the angelus bell had been
the stumps of five dead elms.

Family House

I slept in a room in the roof,
the white planes of its ceiling
freckled with light from the sea,
or at night leaf shadows
from the street-lamp in the lane.

Below, the flame of her hair,
and the gleam of a colander
as she bent among the pea-rows,
or pulled a lettuce from the black earth,
wearing silly shoes to make her taller.

Even in summer, sometimes, salt on the air,
I'd hear far off that faltered heartbeat
of the Breaksea lightship,
then the held breath of silence
to the count of ten.

Now the vegetable garden is a lawn,
and they sold the coach house, pigsty,
the old stable where in wet summers
we crouched over our cache of secrets
under the cidery air of an apple-loft.

From a hundred miles and thirty years away
I smell long rows of fruit,
turned to rotten gourds of juice
soft-skinned as toads.

Stealing Peas

Tamp of a clean ball on stretched gut.
Warm evening voices over clipped privet.
Cut grass. Saltfish from the mudflats,
and the tide far out.

He wore a blue shirt with an Aertex logo,
filthy with syrups of laurel and rhododendron,
the grime of a town park.
We crawled in the pea-rows
in a stolen green light,
pea-curls catching the tendrils of my hair,
peas tight in their pods as sucklers.
We slit the skins with bitten nails,
and slid the peas down the chutes of our tongues.
The little ones were sweet,
the big ones dusty and bitter.

'Who d'you like best?'
Beyond the freckled light of the allotment,
the strawberry beds, the pigeon cotes,
a lawn-mower murmured, and the parky shouted
at a child we could not see.

'You're prettier. She's funnier.'
I wish I hadn't asked.

Sunday

From the mahogany sideboard in the dining-room
she'd unhook the golden question mark
that unlocked her wedding silver,
slide creamy bone from velvet slots,
spoons and forks still powdery with Sylvo,
from their shallow heelprints.

Under the house my father laid his drill,
his ringleted bits, graded and smeared
with a green iridescence of oil.
Screwdrivers, hammers, saws, chisels,
a rising scale, tuned and ready.
Sunday was helping day.

Once, alone for a moment, I saw
the bright nails set for striking.
With my favourite hammer I rang them home.
Some sank sweetly. Some hung sad heads.
Some lay felled, a toehold in the grain.
He stood like thunder at the door.

In the salt-blind dining-room
broken by bells and the silence after,
sprouts steamed sourly in the blue tureen.
The cat mimed at the window.
I levelled myself against the small horizon
of the water jug. The mirrors steadied.

If I kept quiet, my eyes on the jug,
tacking across that loop of water,
the day would mend. They'd nap, separately.
The cat would walk the garden at my heel,
and we'd watch the pond an hour, inching
a stone to the edge, until it fell.

Breakers Yard

Alsatians pick among the bones of Austins.
A mew of blind kittens in the dashboard
of a rusting Ford, butterflies shimmer
over ragwort and red valerian.

Metal and glass ring to the sound of hammers,
and fireweed burns
among miles of breakage,
old engines jammed in an August heatwave.

Bikes drop. We leave them spinning
to clamber the mudguards and bonnets
of old trucks and cars, leap from roof to roof,
stepping-stones too hot to stand on.

It sings like traffic crawling Brooklyn Bridge
in Saturday movies,
or humming the 8-lane freeways
of television.

I take the wheel of a grounded yellow Vauxhall
at the yard's bright heart
and burn headlong into the afternoon
till you scream for mercy.

Sometimes, driving the overpass,
I catch the eye of a mirror from the wreckers yard,
but never, now, a blue bicycle wheel,
its blurred spokes slowing.

The Loft

A ladder strung with webs
stepped out of summer
into harp-strings of light,
apple-breath, the slow let of saps
and a distilling dark.

I pressed my ear to the floor
for the sounds in the drum:
waterfall, generator, a scream of swifts,
the bull knocking his stall,
beasts shifting down below.

Sometimes in the heat
under broken slate
an apple burst,
something scuttled in the grain,
or a swift flung down its glove.

Now, paddling, or dipping my wrists,
I feel corn's gleaming bracelets,
those hands that cooled a fever,
or barred the black angel
whose feather turns on a thread of air.

Hay

Seven hold their breath,
their full arms itch with gleanings.
In the shadow of their hats
their patient faces hurt.

Under the weight of the sky
three horses hang their heads
at the slackened harness,
her hand tense on the bridle.

Not a cloud sails on,
not a leaf stirs. No
movement of air
in the long grass.

Only the skin of a horse
that shivers off the flies,
and the flick of an ear
will tell they lived: only their absences,

blurred flank, a rubbed-out ear,
the photographer in his black hood,
show still like negatives, in every field
where hay was cut.

Beudy[1]

Above my desk the western light selects
a mountain landscape. All afternoon
it lights on lithographs, the sea in oils,
my daughter's pencil drawing of a horse.

The dog sighs in her dream.
Out there a buzzard mews
drawing her blue across the field
where the frost ebbs.

Rose, ink, carmine
rugs from Afghanistan,
the camel-bag from Bukhara
with a glitter of sand still in it.

This room, where beasts were once,
she leaned her cheek against the old cow's flank,
stiff hands warmed at the udder,
the milk singing.

Where the yard door was, hills, a field's far gold,
a white horse like a flake of snow.
Sometimes my foot, treading a deep piled rug,
feels cobblestones, a thin veil of straw.

*

Stillness of clocks. A wren in the ash-tree.
My hands run on the keys.

Words are stones
skipping the page of the screen,

fragments of ice on the morning bucket,
the ring of milk on zinc.

---

[1]   beudy: cowhouse (Welsh)

At dawn, by the windy light of a Tilley lamp,
she warms raw knuckles to pain in cattle breath.

Listening to the beat of the cow's heart
she hauls for milk in black December.

A fever burns her. Hunger's an old dog
whining at her door.

My spaniel sleeps on the Indian rug.
The screen swallows my words, straws in the wind.

Walking on Water

The man who walked on water
from his pretty yacht
is brought from the slippery sea
solemn in a noose of weed.

Whatever was on his mind
as the wave licked him clean
as a bone from the deck
he wrote on the dark sea

with his black breath.
Had anyone been there
they could not have read it
by starlight.

His word gleamed a moment
on the empty sea, by dawn
stretched, illegible
to the world's rim,

and the gulls cried at something
sliding between the leaves of the sea,
lifted, limp into the sky
in the claws of a helicopter.

The West Window of York Minster

Laid out for burial,
a window's bones,
like an old sheep
in shallow snow.

Lacework of stone where, once,
the mason looked up,
chafing his calloused palms
with a grasshopper sound;

where the glazier filled his mind
with carmine, indigo;
where the organist turned after the Agnus Dei,
his hands in his lap;

where the bishop glanced at the westering sun
before Compline,
easing his mind beyond his heavy purples
to his evening draft of wine;

where the bride, lifting her head,
counted out the day;
where the widow raised her eyes
before nightfall, and the fist of earth.

St Winefride's Well

Overhead the wren builds
in the ruined mudcup of the swallow
and a stone pilgrim bears another
on his shoulder. I sip at the step
like an animal at a waterhole.

Here water swallows itself
unravelling its knotwork between ice-ages,
as the sea's slippery pages
turning forever
at the edge of the mind.

It flowers with a small sob
on a powerful stem from a tap-root deep
in a broken earth, a pulse
almost flesh, when the scalpel reveals
the drumming loneliness of the heart.

Just to look is healing,
to stand in the porch of summer
and stare through turbulence
into the dark.

Coming Home

after teaching a poetry course

A week away and I'm coming home.
At five the car breaks dawn in a surf of balsam,
untangles the hill, the lanes, the B-roads.
Stone towns of northern England stir
for the milk and the post.

Bill, his dying wife in his arms a month ago:
Lincolnshire spreads fields of widening gold
about his empty house, sons, daughters,
grandchildren in the sleeping farms,
her shadow cooling in the double bed.

The motorway straightens through the eyes of bridges.
Dawn burns off its gasses over Manchester,
and Sarah's broken childhood bleeds again,
her father's love gone sour and retracted to a vice
that turns the safe-house dead, and blind, and mute.

South on the M6, sunrise in my mirror
dazzles with tears the distant border country.
Into Wales, and for once I dare drive fast
where the road steps off between mountains into air,
Glaslyn blue and silk beyond it.

Jane with her love simpler than marriage
and all pain lost in the simple fact of it,
her body a harp now that the wind stirs.
Tracey, half a mind on poetry, half on visions,
still frail as glass from the doctor's silences.

Home through waking villages, Bala yawns and rises.
Llyn Tegid takes a white sail in its palm.
Anne, after lifelong marriage, keeps house alone,
its rooms about her like his shrugged-off coat,
rehearses in my mind our house, one day.

The lane narrows and turns between sunburnt fields.
Two hundred miles behind me, you at the door
rising for breakfast, a late dream in your eyes.
The slate's already hot. The bees are in the fuchsia.
A rug of sunlight's on the bedroom floor, ours
and the widower's bed spread cool for homecoming.

The Wind-Chimes

after a slate sculpture by Howard Bowcott

A light southerly
fingers the harp on the house-wall
in the heat of May,
careful as ewe's foot and lamb's
stepping their delicate octave
over the waste tips of Blaenau.
A ghost's breath
in the worker's shack above Llanberis
trembles the quarry.

Today heat runs its hands
over the purples, ochres, blues
of slag shards.
A bee blunders into it,
heavy with honey as a belled cow.
An orangetip settles,
her wings' heat-shimmer
adds a small vibration to the tuning
of a cuckoo in a far wood.

From sunrise to afternoon
the wind harp drinks the sun,
notes slowly giving to mellowness.
We play it, absently,
going in and out of the old house, woken
amazed by the sweetest spring in half a century,
an outburst of blossom on ancient trees,
a spool of heat on far hills,
the warm stones singing.

The King of Britain's Daughter

The giant Bendigeidfran, also known as Brân, son of Llŷr, was king of the island of Britain. Matholwch, king of Ireland, married Branwen, daughter of Llŷr. For a year she was happy, until the Irish court became troubled by an old grievance against Wales. Matholwch's brothers demanded vengeance and Branwen was driven from the King's chamber to work in the kitchens. There she reared a starling and taught it to speak her name, and it flew to Wales to find her brother. When he knew of her sorrow, Bendigeidfran set off in rage across the Irish sea with a fleet of ships. In the ensuing battle all but seven men were killed. Branwen was brought home to Wales, where she died of grief.

1   *Rocking Stone*

On the headland is an absence
where it fell some winter night
between here and childhood,
and the sea's still fizzing
over a bruise that will not heal.

A finger would rock it,
Bendigeidfran's stone.
My ear pressed to its flank could hear
the footfall of a storm far out at sea
long before the frown of it darkened the beach.

It purred in wind, was warm against my back
with all the summer in it.
Apple out of legend,
slingstone of Brân's rage against Ireland.
Or so my father said.

2

We'd sing for a bit,
the western sun in our eyes.
Then rocked to sleep in the dark for a hundred miles,
my face in his coat, soft growl
of the Austin in my dreaming bones,

I'd wake suddenly in a turning lane,
the scut of rabbits in the headlights,
the glint of two churns on the stand,
a rutted track over fields,
two gates that had to be opened and closed again.

Then the deep cloud-cold of a feather bed,
mirrors that bloomed with a damp off the sea,
and under the oak bed in the black cave
where the ghost was, and a fleece of dust,
the po, with its garland of roses.

3

Above the house a cat's-tail rises from the fire
his mother lit a generation back.
Beneath her plum-trees air takes up the slack
in someone else's sheets. At dusk

she'll gather their cloudiness off the evening sea,
indoors, cast one and watch it settle
for the keel of her iron to plough,
her glasses misting in a hiss of starch.

4

Seal's head in water.
Brân's footprint in a slab of rock
deep enough for a child to swim.
An ess of light as far as Ireland.
Salt in my mouth and the wind to lean on.
The boom and suck in the cave
where the boat rowed us into the dark
for us to shout.

5

His hat covered my eyes
and his coat dragged in the grass,
the pockets too deep to fathom.

When she gave it away

– it was old, the tweed threadbare,
the gold words faded like old books
inside the headband –

she gave away mornings of forage,
beachcombings, blackberries, pebbles, eggs,
field-mushrooms with pleated linings,

his fist working it to a form
for the leveret that quivered under my hand
before it died.

6

When the world wobbled
we heard it on a radio chained
by its fraying plait of wires
to the kitchen window-sill
between a sheaf of letters,
bills and things needing to be done,
and a jar of marigolds.
And over its Bakelite crown
the sea, level as milk.
The news came out of the sky,
a mist off the sea,
an incoming shadow
of rain or wings.

7

Gorse, knowing no season
of war or winter or times
not flowering, not kissing,
was always yellow,
a burning bush all summer,
but in winter just
one unblinking eye,
a small flame dreaming in a bush
before they fired it,
and the whole cliff burned.

8

Beached for good on the high-tide line,
the houseboat leaned to sea,
at odds with the level earth
in its ballast of stones
and fishy drifts of sand.

Cargo of cuttlefish,
bladderwrack, blue mussels,
the horn of a unicorn,
the skull of a curlew
and maps for the journey,

the King of Britain's daughter
making for open sea
past headlands like drinking dragons,
marked by that neolithic stone
from the giant's pocket.

9

Giants

turn boulders into grains of sand,
a brimming horizon to a goblet,
capstone and orthostats of the cromlech,
a milking stool set slant
on the hill's shoulder.

They loll on skylines,
their heads in the clouds,
warming their bluestone bones in the sun.
They tilt the earth, bring storms
when they breathe like rain on the sea.

They are the metaphors that shift the world,
make delta, Gulf Stream, sea-road
from a stream spilt on the beach,
and turn a houseboat full of sand
to quinquereme on a running tide.

Tonight, as Concorde folds her tern-wings back
to take the Atlantic,
I hear a giant foot stamp twice.
You can still see the mark he made,
a black space in the stars.

10

I swim far out.
Black cliffs rise sheer out of green water
where light is blond over drowned sand,
crevices secret in their mermaid hair.
Sand-martins touch and go, electric,
as if sunlight made rock burn.

I'm cold as sand. In the cave's throat
a breath of samphire, the sunken wreck
in which I'm trapped in dreams
where, in a fishtail gleam
she leans to kiss me as she goes
dressed in her glamour to a Christmas dance.

    A shark descends the staircase of the liner
    and the dancers cannot hear me.

The tide lifts and lets go. Nothing
breaks the surface of darkness or sea
where we beached the boat so long ago,
and I suddenly knew she slipped him,
that he carried like an X-ray
her shadow picture.

    A staircase in the sea
    and something gleaming in the deepest water.

11 *Radio Engineer*

i THE HEAVYSIDE LAYER

Staring into the starry sky, that time
in the darkest dark of war and countryside,
'What is the stars?'
my father asked,

then told me that up there,
somewhere between us and Orion,
hangs the ionosphere, lower, closer at night,
reflecting his long wave signals back to earth,

light bending in water.
But things get tight and close,
words, music, languages
all breathing together under that old carthen,

Cardiff, Athlone, Paris
all tongue-twisted up,
all crackle and interference,
your ears hearing shimmer

like trying to stare at stars.

ii BEDTIME

You'd plan for it, set out equipped,
warmed in and out before you left the fire
for the dash up the dark stairs.
Hot milk, hot water bottles, coats on the bed.
The quickest way to get warm
was to make yourself small,
to pinch shut the edges
of flannelette, carthen, eiderdown, coats,
to breathe in the stuffy cave till you fell asleep
under the breathless weight of the Heaviside layer,
and woke, stunned, into a crowing light.

iii

With wires, transmitters, microphones,
my father unreeled his line

to cast his singing syllables at the sky,
unleashed and riding airwaves up and up

to touch and be deflected,
moths at a silver window in the air.

I saw it, a cast line falling back
through shaken light above the pool,

sound parting water
like a hare in corn.

iv

Outside in the graveyard
I collected frozen roses,
an alabaster dove with a broken wing
for my hoard in the long grass,

while he unreeled his wires down the aisle,
hitched a microphone to the pulpit
and measured silence with a quick chorus
from the *Messiah*.

Still I can't look at stars,
or lean with a telescope, dizzy, against the turning earth,
without asking again, 'What is the stars?'
or calling 'Testing, testing' into the dark.

i

When the King of Ireland
tired of me

they took my child
my velvet and my gold,
my place at table,
my peace, my grace,
my bed of goosedown,
my maid,
my husband,
my heavy crown.

They gave me the scullery,
the servants' cruelty,
a stone floor,
a bed of straw.

ii

I wake suddenly in the dark
as if the world lurched, to hear
in the perpetual sound of waves
an outcry and the growl of war.

Dawn comes over the sill as if
great flares were burning far away
in my drowned country, the rising sun
on the wall like a crock of marigolds.

Oh, my face is salt,
my anger the flung sea.
Under my fist the waves are wild swans
beating out of black mountain lakes.
The spume flies up before my thighs,
serpents and burning flags and tattered sails.

iii

The sun comes to me
from that invisible shore,
like the stones he used to skim for me
across the water.

Pebble of amber,
it rests a moment on the sill
of the sea before describing
its long, slow arc.

If I could walk home
over the water, stepping
on the sun's skim-stones without drowning,
without burning.

Now is the bay turned scullery
where they pluck the geese.
I stamp deep pools into the black slabbed shore,
I lap the earth's tectonic plates,
like folding bones of a baby's skull,
and pleat the great cliffs in my raging hands.

iv

Day after day
a starling comes to my hand,
both of us small birds at a window
he, with a dark rainbow
in every feather, takes seed
and crumbs from me,
touches my hand like rainfall

and I tell my name until
he holds its two syllables
of water in his throat
two pearls to bear across the sea

on a prevailing westerly.
I throw him into the wind
calling 'Branwen, Branwen'
to the far horizon.

Now stone and water rise,
the bay scatters with brokenness.
Wrecks in the deepest sea will crack
their carapaces under my foot.
My ships are gull feathers
towed over the drowned rocks of my rage.

v

When my eloquent starling leaves my hand
I grieve alone, and for a month or more
my eyes never leave the grey and empty sea.

Then when the wind cries all night on the land,
huge waves breaking on the troubled shore,
I wake to hear my child cry in my dream.

At dawn swineherds run breathless to the King
with tales of an island, trees, two lakes, all
moving shoreward on the morning swell.

There, through the littoral, my brave Brân striding,
his tall fleet dancing at his heel
like giddy hounds at a huntsman's beck and call.

I wear the shallows of the littoral
which the long days have warmed. They steady me.
I bridle the currents, wear the sea's cold iron
for armoury, shoulder the hawsers of my fleet
and set out through the sea to Ireland,
taking the west wind to my heart like grief.

vi

When he hears my name
he comes as a black crow,
blessed and iridescent
in the rising sun,
giant striding the sea,
prince with his fleet of ships,
brother with a starling
cupped in his nesting hands.

12   *Branwen's Grave*

Lace of a winter ash-tree
in a broken mirror
where the river strums its stones,
combing and combing
its long green hair.

There is weeping here
in the cold stream,
in the crumpled face of water,
in the sob of wind,
in a cry of water-birds.

There's a whirr of air
and a tambourine of birds
rings in a cold sky,
and the ash is leafed again,
the starling tree.

Her memory erased
from the stones
by the wind and rain,
her name
on the tongue of a bird.

14

Wind's in the limekilns, hollow-eyed,
blind with nettles and pebbles.
Above the spilt light of the stream
the houseboat lolled in the stones,
horizon askew. Spiders wove their latitudes
and longitudes across the porthole.

Day after day we put to sea on a drift of sand,
baling rain from the hull with a tin can,
the hold full of pebbles, oranges,
a glass-stoppered bottle of dandelion burdock,
the *Beano* for the long hours on watch,
the bathers my mother knitted from unpicked cardigans.

Always the skew horizon, and a cave-breath
of salt and fish and rot that I still catch
with a shiver of pleasure.
Day after day we sailed the weather west,
dreaming of Bendigeidfran
towing his rage through the sea.

There's not a plank left,
but round the headland where the stone fell,
black rocks shelve, and the rising tide
drowns the print where his great foot stamped.
In a slither of muscle and fins, the grey Atlantic
settles to green in the arms of the bay.

Today I swim beyond the empty headland
in search of the giant's stone.
Do I see it through green translucent water,
shadow of a wreck, a drowned man's shoulder,
a clavicle huge as a ship's keel
wedged between rocks?

15

The sea writes on the sand
in a scribble of weed and gullbones,
binder twine, coke cans, torn nets,
fish-hooks, broken glass, bladderwrack,
a freehand of mermaid hair and sea-ribbon,
polystyrene chip-trays, spatulas, flip-flops
and sometimes the drowned.
It discards, draft after draft,
each high tide a deadline.

16

When I took you there,
a pebble of basalt in my pocket,
I showed you the white farm, the black beach,
the empty headland where the stone
balanced its mass so delicately,
four thousand years withstanding weather
like a dozing horse.

Walking the beach
we felt the black grains give
and the sun stood
one moment on the sea
before it fell.

Index of Titles

Index of First Lines